I CAN
BUY ANY
CANDY
BAR

To My Dear Friend C.J,

I am delighted to share
my story with you!
And ooooo Thank-You for
being a good friend!

Greg
Nov 2020

I CAN BUY ANY CANDY BAR

An ORDINARY MAN'S
SEARCH *FOR* MEANING

GREG LANCASTER

Printed in the United States of America

First Edition 20 21 22 23 24 25 POL 5 4 3 2 1

CONTENTS

PREFACE

I t is my earnest desire that you discover great benefit from the pages of this book. That being said, I am an ordinary person, just like the majority of people. I am not famous, nor have I held public office. I've not won an Olympic medal, made it to a billionaire club, or hosted an afternoon television talk show. Most of you and I have a lot in common—we are genuinely commonplace folks whose dream is to live life to the fullest and with purpose. I wrote *I Can Buy Any Candy Bar* to pull together many of my life experiences and lessons learned along the way, and share them along with the precious nuggets I have unearthed from some profound books I've read over the years. My goal was to produce a short, concise, fun-to-read book that contains every meaningful thing I have learned and, in the process, provide stimulation and motivation for you to examine your own life as you pursue greater significance, meaning, and joy.

As we go about our day-to-day living, I believe it is absolutely vital to set aside moments to pause and declutter both our thoughts and our schedules. It is important to fully engage our minds to refocus and reposition ourselves regularly and stay committed to what is truly important; otherwise, life just seems to get off-track. Doing so has certainly been a fruitful experience for me.

When I was a youngster, nothing captured my delight and imagination quite like the anticipation of acquiring and eating a candy bar. I think it's because, not only did I love eating them, it was a pleasure that only happened on occasion—it certainly wasn't an everyday occurrence. But wow! I imagined that one day I might be able to buy a candy bar any time I pleased. Could life possibly get *any* better than that?! But even in my early years of candy bar delight and gratification, I sensed that one day life would be even grander. *Someday,* I thought, *something even better than a candy bar will be the center of life's fulfillment.* Even then, I sensed that my childhood pleasures would one day transform into more grown-up types of things. I eventually learned that sometimes, obstacles get in the way of the simple things that bring real joy.

Life and how we choose to live it is a crucial matter. To take life lightly and to live it without a central, guiding purpose is not wise. Deep down within our inner being, we want to have greater significance and meaning, but we don't know how to attain it. To live a life that really matters—to be someone who makes a real difference in the world—is a desire that dwells deep within us. When we choose to live without vision or mission, we open ourselves up for "could have been" regrets that plague many of us. Essentially, we often settle for less—far less—than for what we were created.

My hope is that this book will encourage and stir you to embrace living a life of significance and abundant joy. Remember, you have only one life to live. Trust me when I say, you don't want to look back and lament over how it was squandered. It is also very important to know that your life does indeed matter. Without embracing this understanding, life is truly meaningless.

The pages before you are my account of living an examined life, with my eyes and mind wide open all the way. Be encouraged.

1

TOWN DAY

Mom went into town every Friday morning like clockwork, as Friday was grocery day. There were thirteen of us kids (I was number eight), and we each longed for "our turn" to go with her. Obviously, we didn't get out much. When school was out in the summer, this was one of the few anticipated opportunities for my brothers, my sisters, and me to leave the farm, even if it was only for a couple of hours.

Town day also meant a candy bar day. Mom would buy each of us a candy bar of our choice at Ross's IGA store—that's why we all lobbied for our turn. Whoever went with her had the opportunity to choose which kind of candy bar she would buy. If I went, a PayDay or Snickers was the choice. How could anything possibly be better? If my sister Ronda went, you could be sure a 3 Musketeers bar would be the treat of the week. Now, I've never had a candy bar that I didn't like, even a 3 Musketeers, but who on God's green earth would choose a 3 Musketeers bar over the likes of a PayDay or Snickers? Sure, a 3 Musketeers bar is larger, but the advantages stop right there. Ronda could have chosen at least one of my two favorites. Or why not a Zagnut, Zero, or Bit-O-Honey? Even a Milky Way*? In any case, even if we didn't know which bar we'd get, one thing was always predictable: Friday was town day and that meant a candy bar, regardless of the selection.

It's nearly impossible to put into words just how much a candy bar on town day really meant to me. I relished the entire event—the build-up in my mind, the anticipation, the purchase, and, finally, the moment of consumption. Happiness and fulfillment were obtained. There was nothing else I could imagine that would match the excitement. I'm sure my brothers and sisters felt similar enthusiasm, but to what extent I'm not sure. You see, back then, a candy bar was a very personal form of happiness for me, and each week, it took on its own different meaning—a unique contribution to my existence. Life was simpler then, but not always easy or comfortable, so even the smallest treat made life a little better.

I grew up on a small, hilly piece of farmland in southeastern Indiana, and, as I said, I was born smack dab in the middle of fifteen children—two of whom died as infants. By the time a candy bar defined happiness for me, my oldest brother and sister had already left home and my three youngest siblings were not yet born. My father worked second shift in a factory nearly an hour from home. He also sustained and operated our small dairy farm, where we also raised hogs and chickens and grew enough grain and hay to feed them all. Of course, Mom and us kids helped out as much as we could.

Corn was picked and stored right on the farm in a corn crib.

Two or three times a week, my brother Randy and I would shovel a truckload of corn for Dad to take to the feed mill for processing the following morning. When school was in session, we were never able to ride along with him to the feed mill unless he went on Saturday morning. When that happened, our excitement nearly matched Friday's town day with Mom.

The feed mill didn't have candy bars, at least not to my recollection. What it did have, however, was cold Nehi soda pop in a long neck glass bottle, and on a hot, humid Indiana day inside a dusty feed mill, a frosty bottle of Nehi took on its own candy-bar-like meaning. I don't know that Randy or I ever really talked about why we always wanted to go to the feed mill, but Dad would often pull just the right amount of loose change from the front pocket of his bibbed overalls and plunk it into the soda pop machine. There I stood as a young boy already burdened with decisions—would it be orange or grape? As I reached in and withdrew my selection from the machine, another bottle would quickly replace the position mine had occupied. Then, Randy would have his choice to make.

I don't remember ever asking Dad for a Nehi soda or for money to put into the machine. We just didn't do things like that back then—no nagging or whining. Sometimes Dad walked by the pop machine in that dark, dusty hallway and deposited money, and sometimes he didn't. Of course, we were disappointed if there was no Nehi that day, but there was always next time, so a new enthusiasm was quickly fueled for the next trip to the feed mill. Maybe not getting a bottle of soda pop every time was a deliberate action on his behalf. If he had coughed up the money every time and we expected it each trip, it would not occupy such a special place in my memories today.

Many years later, I recalled hearing a conversation between my dad and Uncle Ray one afternoon underneath the black locust tree in the side lawn. I remember nothing of the specific nature of the conversation, only that Dad ended the discussion with the statement, "The more people have, the more people complain." Maybe that is why Randy and I didn't get treated to a Nehi on each trip to the feed mill and why we had only limited opportunities to visit the grocery store on town day with Mom.

Why do these events hold such a special meaning for me now? Would a candy bar really be that spectacular if you had one anytime you had the craving?

I think we both know the answer to that. Looking back, I know there were times—many times—my parents just couldn't afford a candy bar or Nehi for us kids, and deep down I knew it. But not having something every time I wanted it helped me to dream and envision a day in the future when I could walk into any store and purchase anything I wanted without fear of ending the week with empty pockets. To place things in proper perspective, I had no images of large, lavish purchases; just the basics, like a candy bar—any kind, any time I wanted.

As a boy, I had only limited opportunities to visit a store, even if I had a nickel, a dime, or the mother lode of all finds, a quarter. As I grew older, there were more opportunities to go, but I still had the frustration of having no money. I often imagined a day when life would be grander, richer, and more fulfilling—a day I could walk into any store and stroll by the candy counter to buy whatever I wanted. I knew this day would eventually come, but when?

One overcast summer day, Randy and I lay across the bed in our shared upstairs bedroom with our chins propped on our hands as we gazed to the east toward the barn. Between our bedroom and the barn was the driveway that dropped off the hill and joined the gravel road at the mailbox. From our driveway, the road rose calmly to the east up the hill beyond the barn, between the red cedar trees and the power poles, and disappeared at the top of the hill. The road led away from the farm toward town. We both knew we would leave the farm when we grew up, as our older brothers and sisters had done. We were in elementary school then, but already playing with visions of the future.

Randy and I shared a common vision that day. A few months earlier, Dad made a deal with the kids who helped milk the cows. If the milk check was over a base amount, those of us who helped with the early morning and evening milkings could keep the extra money. For example, if the expected milk check for that week was $100 and the amount of milk sold earned $120, we were able to split the extra twenty dollars equally among us.

This was Dad's way of providing a little reward when the job was done right. You see, there are a lot of factors that influence just how much milk a cow will produce, such as feed, the time of year, and how thoroughly she was milked. A milking session with twenty cows in a tiny three-stanchion barn could take one and a half hours if it was done right, or only one hour if we hurried and did not milk the cows thoroughly and properly. Thus, the milk-check incentive. If we were able to share in the profits, we were less likely to hurry through the milking session. Any hurried, sloppy approach would then be taking money directly from our own pockets. It's amazing how quickly we learned this concept and how quickly we changed poor working habits when a reward was involved.

During the late summer months when the cows were grazing in fresh pasture, they naturally produced more milk, so we always had more money in our pockets. But as winter neared and milk production dropped off, so did the extra money. I must have saved nearly every cent I earned. Sure, I bought a candy bar, bottle of soda pop, or piece of Bazooka bubble gum here and there, but what else was there for me to spend money on anyway? Life looked pretty darn good to me then. It was nice to have some money, because you never knew when you might have the opportunity to go to the grocery store, feed mill, or gas station.

Well, that day in our upstairs bedroom, Randy and I had our vision all figured out. Together, we would own our own dairy farm and milk enough cows to afford to buy a car and a motorcycle, all before we were twenty-five years old. We would be set; it was as simple as that. We would have each other's companionship, wheels to drive or ride, and a little money to spare. What else was there? Life was beginning to take on and form new meaning.

Randy and I never carried out those early childhood dreams, of course. I don't remember any conscious decision made by either of us to choose a different path; we just did. As we grew older, things just changed. Things have a way of doing that—plans change unannounced. No hoopla or fanfare. It happens little by little, sometimes for the best, sometimes not.

The wonderment of childhood is a time that most of us look back on with great fondness and innocence. It is during those years that we are introduced to delights such as town day, candy bars, and soda pop, plus we get our first taste of what it feels like to have a little money in our pockets. We harken back to those years with fondness because we know deep within that a simpler life is a more fulfilling life.

2

CONTENTMENT HAS A NAME: MOM

I don't recall Mom ever wanting anything. Maybe wanting was just a kid thing anyway. Maybe Mom never had time to want anything. After all, taking care of a house full of children and helping with farm chores was a full-time commitment. I remember when Mom would help with the morning milking and get back to the house to fix breakfast for all of us—and I mean a real meat, eggs, and biscuits breakfast, not a bowl of cold cereal, bagel, or cup of yogurt. Then she would wake up the rest of the younger kids and get all of us ready for school and on the bus, all before 7:00 a.m. She repeated this routine day after day after day.

Mom was certainly not unfamiliar with work; she had worked hard her entire life. She was from a large family of ten children and grew up on a farm before modern mechanization such as tractors, corn-pickers, hay balers, and automatic milking machines were widely available. She had to drop out of school after graduating the eighth grade because there was important work to do at home and on the farm. I recall her telling me how, as a teenager, she would work in the cornfields every day during late spring and early summer, cutting weeds and hoeing corn by hand. By the time her siblings were old enough to look after themselves, she was fortunate to be able to earn money working for neighboring farmers rather than working at home for no pay. I vividly remember her telling me the workdays were usually ten hours long and the pay was around a dollar per day. But it was money nonetheless, and money was hard to come by during the Great Depression. She and her family were grateful for every dollar they could earn.

Immediately after Mom and Dad were married, Dad farmed with her father, or Poppy, as she referred to him. I remember her recalling those early years of marriage and how she sewed and mended gloves every evening by the light of an oil lantern. During the day, Dad and Poppy would shuck corn by hand and wear holes in several pairs of gloves during a single day's work. Each and every fall and early winter evening, until the harvest was complete, Mom ended her day by sewing and mending gloves for the following workday so new blisters might be prevented for just one more day. No, Mom was not unfamiliar with work.

Keeping in mind that I was born right in the middle of fifteen children, I never remember my mother not being pregnant or not caring for a newborn baby. In actuality, that probably wasn't the case, since there is a span of twenty-six years that separate the oldest, Charles Larry, from the youngest, Jeffery Allen. But from my point of view, Mom was not only hard at work with household duties, canning vegetables, and doing farm chores, but she was a full-time mother of little ones year after year after year. I never heard her utter one complaint about all that was laid before her— not once! I also never sensed that Mom ever wanted for anything that she didn't already have. She gave birth to Jeff, the youngest, just two months shy of her forty-seventh birthday. This meant she went through menopause, and all of the associated challenges and physical trials this stage of life presents, with a house full of children to raise and household responsibilities heaped on top of it. My sister Pam recalls clearly how Mom would take just a momentary break from peeling potatoes or doing laundry. She'd sit down on a chair, pull her dress up to her knees, and fan her face with a Look magazine to cool off from the hot flashes. It would only be a few minutes before she'd be right back to her normal work. Years later, as an adult, Pam consulted with Mom about her experiences with menopause and asked her how she had dealt with it, day after day, week after week, year after year. Mother's reply was, "Lord, Pamela Sue, I never had time for menopause. I had too much work to do."

Upon reflection many years later, how was it that Mom had the best sense of humor in the entire family? You would think a woman with so much work with so little visible reward, with only the bare necessities to live and work with, plus the physical wear and tear of birthing fifteen children, would be a worn-down Negative Nellie. By the grace of God, that wasn't the case at all. Mom had a tremendous sense of humor and was just flat-out funny. We were all blessed with her marvelous sense of funniness.

I recall a conversation I had with Mom long after we had all grown up and left the farm. I was talking about how Randy and his family had recently taken a trip to Florida to enjoy Disney World, along with all the fantastic entertainment venues in that area. I had never been to Disney World, but I was still very excited for their opportunity to go, and I shared my enthusiasm with her. I said, "Isn't it great that Randy's family went to Disney World?" Mom's reply was, "Lord, Greg, if Disney World was in my barn lot, I wouldn't walk out there through the gate to see it." I thought that was so hilarious, I almost wet my pants with uncontrolled laughter. Not only was her comment hilarious, but it also spoke to her nature—she was genuinely content in all circumstances.

My goodness, even many years later, Mom's sense of humor was put on display when we were all gathered at the local funeral home when my father passed away. To anyone who has attended a funeral visitation, you are well aware of the swing of emotions. One moment you're in tears, and the next moment you are cheerfully greeting and visiting a relative or friend you haven't seen in years. There was a moment toward the end of the evening when Mom was clearly near exhaustion and leaning on the side of Dad's casket with tears dripping down her cheeks. As several of us drew near and put our arms around her, she looked up, wiped away the tears, began to chuckle, and said, "Jim, I can't believe you're in heaven, and here I am left with these bone spurs and bunions in my aching feet!" Mom simply had a way of making us laugh, regardless of the moment or situation.

Even before I was old enough to begin elementary school, I remember Mom taking a break from her midday chores to sit on the davenport with Ronda on one side and me on the other. We would watch *Queen for a Day* on the television, or she'd read a Bible story to us. The quiet time with her did not come frequently, but it was so very special. As she read the stories of Samson's encounter with a lion, David slaying Goliath, or how Jesus loved all children, her soft, warm arm would be around me and her rough, callused hands would stroke mine. Ronda and I loved those stories. We hung on each word and could visualize a setting far different from our farm where these biblical events had taken place. It all seemed so mystical.

Queen for a Day was Mom's favorite television show. Heck, even I enjoyed it. Each week a group of female contestants would be interviewed about their hardships and the needs that went with them. At the end, the audience would choose a winner, and she'd actually get to wear a crown and a sable robe as her name was announced to viewers. All the women who wore the crown seemed so happy. They'd get red roses and a list of prizes—anything from vacations to kitchen appliances—that were donated to them.

I really wanted Mom to be on that show and be crowned queen for a day. If anyone deserved to wear that crown, it was her. But as the three of us sat there watching the show, not for a moment did I suspect that she ever wanted to be on it, nor did I believe she envied the winning ladies. Maybe she just wanted downtime to get off her feet for a few minutes and be alone with her children. Or perhaps she was doing her part to make precious memories. Even though I was a young boy who adored his mother very much and wanted her to wear that sparkling crown, I'm confident today, now that she has left this world, that she is indeed wearing a crown—but it's an unfading crown of glory.

There is such a thing as supernatural contentment—it is not of this world. Even though I always felt Mom deserved better, perhaps she had already received the very best. By grace, maybe she had been granted far more than I, or anyone else, will ever know.

3

FREE FROM BOREDOM

I was never bored as a child. In fact, if I or one of my brothers or sisters ever professed to being bored, it was news to me. We had chores to do—Mom and Dad saw to that. As a youth, I wasn't a big fan of all the work I had to do, but I definitely appreciated the time off after the work was done. After supper, we all usually had free time to do whatever we chose to do.

During the summer, when the daylight lingered until 9:00 p.m., a game of Kick the Can would be in order, although, it always seemed the game wouldn't start until just before dark, and we'd play well into the night. About dusk, the fireflies—or lightning bugs, as we called them—would sparkle across the lawn with their blinking rear ends. Amongst all the blinking we would race around the corner of the house to hide after sneaking up to kick the can off the end of the sidewalk. If the "can tender" caught a glimpse of you replacing the can to its original position, you were *it*, the new can tender. Being a can tender definitely was not an enviable position.

If we weren't playing Kick the Can, we'd be well involved in a game of kickball, hide-and-seek, or some other invented activity. One of our favorites was to venture down to the woodlot across the large field beside our house and find the perfect grapevine that climbed all the way to the treetops. A tree that supported a large, woody grapevine was quite a find, especially if it was located on a hillside or along the edge of a ravine. The base of such a vine would be well rooted into the ground, so we would have to drag an axe or carry a hatchet into the woods with us to chop off the vine from the soil. This was no easy task, but after several minutes—or hours—of chopping, the vine would be free from the ground and the base of the tree. It was now ready for swinging.

For the first day or so, the vine would feel stiff and not perform quite up to our expectations, but after repeated attempts to swing over the gully or ravine, it would eventually succumb to our pulls and carry us out over the stream and back again safely. A running start down the bank with the vine firmly in hand would produce a magnificent ride out over the edge of the bank and back. I'm not sure that Mom or Dad would have approved of this activity if they had known, but they had other grown-up responsibilities to occupy themselves. They may or may not have known what we were up to then, but they knew we were entertaining ourselves and having fun, the way kids are supposed to. It was nobody's responsibility to entertain us—we entertained ourselves. We used our imaginations, which is what children do when given the chance.

While many games or activities have a season associated with them, in Indiana, *any* season is basketball season. We had a solid iron basketball hoop that we had dug out of a junk pile and placed it inside the barn, outside the barn, inside the corn crib, outside on a pole, or against the woodshed. It seemed we were constantly moving the hoop for one reason or another, but we didn't care so long as we had one.

Here's what I remember most about all of the different locations for the hoop: we hung the hoop ourselves, just my younger brother Randy and me. We never asked Dad or an older brother who might be visiting at the time, to help move the hoop and install it elsewhere; we just did it ourselves. And when you're a fifth grader hanging a basketball hoop with the assistance of your younger brother, things get pretty interesting.

Some of our earliest basketball hoop-hanging jobs weren't the best, to say the least. Once, the hoop was hanging down so loosely, the impact of the basketball tore it off the wall after only a few minutes of shooting. Sometimes the hoop didn't fall completely off the wall, but would simply lean forward for a few days prior to taking its final descent down to the ground. We weren't very talented at carpentry work initially, but we were actively learning along the way. Before we knew it, our next re-hanging job improved over the previous one, and the hoop would stay up for weeks at time before it came tumbling down. As we grew a bit older and wiser, we discovered that lag screws or bolts were far better at holding a basketball hoop in place than nails and baling wire. Bolts didn't pull out of the wall like nails did, so there was much rejoicing on the farm when we finally discovered that! Believe it or not, as we grew older, the height of the basketball hoop actually shortened. It seems as if it should have been the other way around, doesn't it?

A standard basketball hoop is installed ten feet above the floor. As you grow up and become bigger and stronger, you are better able to score on a normal ten-foot goal. But the last and final installation was hung at the height of eight feet, four inches above the floor. This was just the perfect height for Randy and me to imitate Wilt Chamberlain and Bill Russell dunking basketballs and blocking shots left and right. Randy and I, along with our high school buddies, spent hundreds of hours playing, dunking, and hanging from that hoop, game after game, night after night. If it was too cold for the ball to bounce properly, we'd take it inside and place it in the bathtub with hot water to warm it up. Then we'd quickly run back out to the shed to resume playing before the ball could cool down and cease to bounce again. How we could soak our T-shirts and sweatshirts with sweat while playing in the middle of winter is beyond explanation, but we did it, night after night.

Our younger siblings played on that hoop for years after Randy and I grew up and left the farm. They most likely had as much fun as we did on that makeshift basketball court, at least I hope they did. Hopefully each of them has fond memories of the endless hours of fellowship we experienced underneath that hoop. Years later, after all of my younger siblings were grown and left home, Mom granted permission for me, along with my two sons, to remove that solid iron hoop from the shed in Indiana and transport it here to our home in Wisconsin. That hoop is still hanging at our home, installed eight feet four inches above the concrete floor, where it is being enjoyed and memories are still being made by our adult children, grandchildren, and friends.

Several years ago I spoke with my mother—who was seventy-eight years old at the time—about the issue of so many children today who have been denied the privilege of entertaining themselves. Many parents have really done their children an injustice by providing so many toys, gadgets, and activities to entertain them. Oh my! This has really grown to epidemic proportions. It is now commonplace to hear children of our adult friends tell their parents, "I'm bored." So many of these children have every toy under the sun, are enrolled in numerous supervised activities such as soccer, baseball, dance, gymnastics, and karate, *and* have their own smartphone, computer games, laptop or tablet, and a television in their bedroom, and yet they are bored.

Several of our friends' children routinely bring videos or computer games along with them when they come over to visit, even if only for a short time. The videos or computer games serve to keep their children entertained, even for a few precious minutes, so their parents might have the opportunity to converse with other adults without being interrupted. The engaging effect of the video or game is only temporary, however, and within minutes, the child is nagging to Mom or Dad, "I'm bored. When are we going home?" Sometimes parents will even suggest, "Put in another video; we'll be leaving soon."

It appears that many children today do not associate happiness with a candy bar or find pleasure in a game or activity birthed from their own imagination. Happiness may never present itself again to the modern generation of children the way it did to me when I was a child. Many children today are simply bombarded with too many diversions and are therefore incapable of thinking for themselves. Of course, I hold no degrees in child psychology or the like. My only credentials come from being a child myself and helping to raise two sons of my own. I asked my mother, who has successfully raised thirteen children, "Why are we, as a generation of people, doing this to our children? Why are these children so bored?" Mother simply replied, "Children today don't have responsibilities around the home, that's why."

When I grew up, and certainly for all generations before me, whether you lived on a farm or in an urban area, we simply had stuff that we had to do, and everybody helped. Parents assigned us daily work responsibilities or chores. Most were predictable, but some would be different from time to time. When we finished our work, we were afforded the opportunity to do what children do naturally: entertain ourselves. The playtime was granted based on the successful completion of our responsibilities at home. And as I stated earlier, by the time we finished our chores, we *appreciated* our free time to play and have fun. Simple things like eating a candy bar, playing a game outside with friends or family, reading a book, or even watching a favorite TV show should bring a degree of contentment and happiness to a young person. Activities like these should never be boring. I think Mom is right on this one.

4

DAD WAS A THINKER

I 've always been a thinking sort of person—more than most, so I am told. The signature question that I pose to any passenger who finds him or herself seated next to me in a vehicle is, "So, what are you thinking about right now?" They've heard it over and over and over again. My wife is politely accommodating and tells me what's on her mind, but sometimes she gives me "the look" that says, "Seriously? You must be kidding. Can't we just enjoy the drive?" My children or grandchildren, over the years, have tried the usual lazy response: "I don't know . . . nothing." "Nothing!" I quickly respond. "Do you know the definition of 'nothing'? *Nothing* is that which rocks dream about. So unless you are a rock, let's come up with a better response than 'nothing,' okay?" My theory is that it's impossible to think about nothing, so let's talk. My wife has had to bear with this obsessive behavior of mine for forty-three years. Can you believe she hasn't kicked me to the curb somewhere along the line?

My dad was a thinker, so I must have inherited my thinking nature from him. I don't know that Dad ever labored in thought over the big questions in life, but if he did, he never discussed it with me. Dad didn't say a whole lot to me as I was growing up; we didn't have the typical *Leave It to Beaver* father-and-son conversations. Perhaps he was simply just too busy with life, and with me being born right in the middle of a huge pack of children, it just didn't happen.

Each of my brothers and sisters has a different perspective of their relationship with Dad, and that's quite natural, I suppose. The older brothers talk about how he coached their baseball teams and was involved in their lives. After I grew up and left home, I saw him engaged in the lives of my three youngest siblings. But the group of us in the middle of the family missed out on a typical father relationship. During that season, Dad worked the farm in addition to forty to sixty hours a week at a factory job. There was only so much of the man to spread around, and he was spread pretty thin. I'm sure he did as well as he could, considering the circumstances. We always had food on the table, clothes for our backs, shoes for our feet, and a house to call home. We didn't want for any of the necessities of life.

In addition to being a thinker, Dad was a problem solver who could fix or repair anything. Part of that aptitude and skill came from serving in the infantry (he was wounded twice in Luxemborg during WWII and received two Purple Hearts), and part of it came from his training as a certified machine repairman. As a farmer, there's always a problem to solve on some piece of machinery needing repair. I don't recall Dad ever hiring anyone to fix something; he repaired everything himself—I mean *everything*! Some solutions to problems were more difficult and complex than others. On more than one occasion I saw him reach a dead end, and he'd simply put down the tools and walk away. He wasn't giving up, mind you—no, no, a thousand times no! He never gave up on any problem; he just needed time to clear his mind and think about the situation from a different point of view. I've seen him step away from a situation for several days only to come back to it with a fresh, well-thought-out approach for finding an answer. That's what he did to earn a living in the factory and that's what he did on the farm. He had a superior sense of reason and a willingness to humble himself to retreat to a quiet place where he could be alone with his thoughts. This enabled him to deal successfully with nearly all that life threw his way. Dad was a thinker.

Since Dad could seemingly figure out anything on his own, I guess he assumed that I could too. You see, Dad never really explained how to do something; he just said, "Go do it." I don't know if this was intentional parenting or if he just didn't have the time to show us or take time to offer detailed instruction. I clearly recall him coming into the living room one early afternoon, just prior to leaving for his second shift factory job. He took me by the left arm, directed me over to the west window, pulled the drapes aside, and said, "You see that field of corn here west of the house?" I replied, "Yes, I see it." Dad said, "Take the Ford tractor and cultivate that field of corn this afternoon." I was in shock, dumbfounded, and nearly lost for words! I was only twelve years old at the time and had never cultivated a field of corn in my life. Sure, I knew how to drive a tractor, and I had pulled a hay baler and wagon before, but nothing like this. This type of work required much more skill.

All I could think was, *I'm going to run over too many knee-high corn plants at the end of the rows when I turn the tractor around!*

When Dad goes outside tomorrow morning to check my work, I'm going to be in big trouble. So after pausing for a moment, I looked up at him and replied, "Uh, I've never cultivated corn before. I don't even know how to do it." Dad looked at me sternly, yet assuredly, and said, "The first person who ever cultivated corn had never done it either. You'll figure it out." Then he walked out of the living room and into the kitchen, grabbed his metal lunch box, and headed out the back door. That was that!

Well, that afternoon, I nervously took the tractor out and cultivated the field of corn, just like I was told, and I'm certain I knocked down far more corn plants than Dad would have. I didn't sleep well that night and fully expected to hear his criticism the next morning, but he didn't say anything. It was business as usual. I didn't get into trouble like I feared, and I learned, all on my own, how to do something that was above my pay grade at the time.

Looking back, I believe the best lessons in life are learned by figuring things out on your own; by trial and error; by experiencing failure as well as success. Dad had learned that long ago, and he was simply imparting that knowledge and wisdom on to me. I didn't understand this at twelve years old, but over my life I've reflected back on that experience many times and the lessons I learned. Dad was a thinker who knew exactly what he was doing and why he was doing it. I understand now that I've inherited some of that hardwiring from him, and I'm thankful I did.

Growing up on a farm presented me with a ton of opportunities to learn new things, connect with the outdoor environment, and enjoy adventures that most city kids didn't have. Even though all of us children immensely enjoyed our fun time off, none of us were fond of the day-after-day work and chores that came with it. So whenever one of us had an opportunity to leave, whether for an overnight stay at sister Betty's or a weeklong stay at Uncle Ray's, we jumped at the chance. I guess that goes to show that, even in our youth, we desire change in our lives, a diversion from daily routines. There's an old saying I'm sure you've heard: "The grass is always greener on the other side of the fence." It seems we aren't content in any season or age, are we? I once heard Nancy L. DeMoss comment on a radio broadcast, "If you are not content with what you have, you will never be content or satisfied with what you want." Hmmm. I think she's on to something.

In hindsight, having a father who invested in me by letting me do things and figure things out on my own was a huge blessing. Witnessing firsthand my Dad's superior sense of reason and my mother's contentment would one day help shape the adult I hoped to become.

5

TRUTH: THE SEARCH BEGINS

Having the ability to think logically and thoroughly served me well during the transition from childhood—and the wonderment of it all—to the teenage/young-adult years. It was time I began the search for truth and significance in my life. Even as an adolescent, my thinking was in the philosophical and spiritual realm. I have always been one who ponders things. I heard more than once while growing up, "It's not that big of a deal, Greg. You think too much, just go with the flow." I thought about lots of things while growing up, from candy bars and soda pop to why so many political leaders were being assassinated and why the Vietnam War lingered on so long.

The more confusing life became, the more I needed and searched for real, objective truth. What was truth, anyway? If something was true for me, did that mean it was true for everyone else? I couldn't let these questions go until I settled them within my inner being. I often wondered, *Is something true because I say it's true, or is it true because of some higher moral standard? Does God decide what is true and what is not true? Which god do we look to, anyway?*

As I grew older, things changed. The wonderment of childhood was amazing but fantasies of the next town day or candy bar no longer satisfied all of my yearnings as I approached the adolescent years. Activities like basketball, baseball, jumping bicycles off homemade ramps, and swinging from grapevines were exciting and quenched the thirst for newfound moments of happiness, but they were for children, and I was no longer a child. I was now noticing many things that felt and looked wrong in the world, and I wondered how mankind had made such a mess of things.

The questions kept flooding in. *Why are so many talented, young musicians killing themselves with drug overdoses? Why don't black people have the same privileges and opportunities I enjoy? Why are there so many poor people around the world who can't afford food and decent clothing while other people have too much of everything? Why doesn't this "Jesus" character return to earth and rid the world of all the injustice, war, pestilence, and grief? Doesn't the Bible promise that something like this is supposed to happen? Where is God in all this suffering? Does God even exist? Mom promised he did. Folk singers and modern ballad writers have recorded songs about these things—maybe because they know the answers and have it all together? Maybe the world needs another Bob Dylan. Maybe that's what I'll do when I grow up and leave home.*

My mind was constantly occupied with life's big issues such as injustice, the environment, the plight of the poor, racial inequality, meaning in life, and God. Who was this God that Mom spoke of so fondly, anyway? Songs like "Blowin' in the Wind" and "The Times They Are A-Changin'" spoke to my heart and demanded that I not be concerned with trivial things that other teenagers engaged in. I had a greater purpose in life and a greater reason to live than to simply grow up, get a decent job, make a comfortable living, and buy my favorite candy bar any time I wanted. I was sure I was to do great things with my life once I discovered exactly what that looked like. I was searching for significance and how I was to wrap my arms around it, and what to do with it once I found it. There had to be more to life than a candy bar, right?

I think I grew up a little earlier than most of my high school classmates. I don't mean to boast that I was more mature, but I was ready for high school to be over a few years early. So when it was finally over, I began taking college classes at a nearby Indiana University field campus and started working a third shift factory job. The night job allowed me to take a full load of late afternoon and early evening classes, do a little studying, head to work at 11:00 p.m., get home by 8:00 a.m. the following morning, clean up and catch some sleep, then do it all over again for the remainder of the week. That was my routine for two years. Mixed in between all of that, I found opportunities for some down time on the weekends or during semester breaks.

Even with a fairly busy schedule during the week, my friend Ted and I hung out a little and talked about some of the bigger issues in life. I believe I first met Ted in a freshman-level philosophy class. We became really good friends right off the bat. We had similar interests, viewpoints, and concerns for things that were wrong in the world. We could sit around for hours and talk about current issues or listen to songs, and sometimes Ted would fill me in on the latest book he'd just finished reading. He was a voracious reader and could devour a whole book in a single day. We would, at times, have silly contests like who could go the longest without sleep. I thought I had a built-in advantage since I worked all night, and as long as I kept busy during the day, I had the greater chance at winning. But Ted would read all night to stay awake. That was the strangest thing I had ever heard. For heaven's sake, if I'm the least bit tired and open a book, I'm out in a minute. But the written word spoke to Ted's heart and soul in a way I had never experienced. Reading awakened him from head to toe. He was a thinker like me, but what set us apart was, he could stay awake for more consecutive hours than I could, and he did it by reading the night away.

It was common then, and probably still is today, for thinking young adults to develop close relationships and bonds while mulling over the bigger points in life. This brings to mind an obscure song by Bob Dylan titled "Bob Dylan's Dream." I encourage you to go online to view the lyrics or listen to the song. Dylan sings of a time when he and his friends gathered often to discuss and think about the big questions in life, and how they might participate in making this world a better place to live. The song also hints at simpler times when friendships were cherished and fellowship was meaningful and satisfying to the soul. It speaks of how the busyness of life tends to get in the way of those relationships, and before you know it, friends disappear one by one. Dylan ends the song longing for those times, wishing to return to those gatherings and friends. He cries out that he'd give thousands of dollars in an instant if he could return to the good ole days.

I don't know if this strikes a chord with you, but it certainly does with me. It speaks to a time of our first budding, meaningful adult friendships and the dreams that we shared. It speaks of a time when things were simpler and had more clarity; a time when we longed for less and felt more satisfied. It also speaks to a longing in our hearts to return to that time and to those relationships. It testifies to how life just gets in the way of our noble dreams and how close friendships sometimes fall victim to circumstances, choices, and time. Change happens, sometimes with no great fanfare or warning—it just happens. And as the years go by, we realize our lives are completely different from what we used to dream and talk about, and there's a longing to return—if even for a short while—to revisit those times.

Ted was an usher in my wedding when I married just prior to my junior year of college. Within a month after the wedding, Vicky and I moved to West Lafayette, Indiana, where I began classes at Purdue University. Ted and I remained in contact for a while via an occasional letter or telephone call, but it wasn't long before each of us was doing life without the other. We just lost touch with one another. There was no conscious decision on my part or Ted's part not to have a relationship; it just happened. Sometimes, things just happen. I haven't spoken with Ted in over forty years.

I was the first member of my family to graduate from college with a bachelor's degree. This spoke more to the changing times we were living in rather than any superior accomplishment or calling on my part. The economy was changing, and you could no longer just graduate from high school and get a good, reasonably paying job. When you look across the whole spectrum of all my brothers and sisters, oldest to youngest, the younger half received more formal education, whereas the older half were the higher income earners. There's a bit of irony there, don't you think? I've found that initiative, drive, hard work, and the relentless pursuit of a goal are the characteristics of financially successful people. In most cases, their level of formal education has very little to do with attaining financial success.

During college and immediately after receiving my degree, I worked full-time in a factory, since a position in my chosen profession was hard to come by. Being a thinking person and a bit mechanically inclined, I enjoyed most of my time in a manufacturing setting. Some of the jobs were better than others, of course, but none of them were boring or meaningless. I worked some menial jobs, but soon progressed to machine operator positions, where the pay was better, and so were the challenges. I was even a foreman during one of my stints. The best thing about my factory working days were the people I was privileged to work alongside. They were hardworking, dependable, fun to be around, and dedicated leaders in their families and communities. They, along with the farming community, formed the backbone of America at that time.

One of the reasons I enjoyed factory work so much is that I knew I wouldn't be working in the same place for the next forty-five years. Despite the dedication and fun spirit I experienced with many of my coworkers, I saw that look on their faces that said, "I'm stuck here until something better comes along, or until I'm worn out and can no longer lift my required items, or until I die or retire from this place." There was also a spirit of resignation among many who worked in the same hot, dirty, noisy plant each and every day. I could work there quite joyfully for the short term, but I anticipated much more than making a career of it. I saw what it had done to my dad over the years and had heard through Ted what it had done to his dad. Deep down, I felt there had to be more to life than factory work, and I wanted to find it.

Well, the two-plus years I spent at Purdue finishing my degree were a blur. I had changed majors and needed to take on extra classes in order to graduate on time. I continued to work part-time and full-time jobs along the way in order to pay for school and ordinary life expenses. By that time, I had left behind my child-hood and adolescent friends; they seemed to be a distant, faded memory. Those relationships had certainly been essential and key to providing meaning in life before, but they were slowly replaced with different relationships and new loves.

By the time I graduated college, Vicky and I were a family of three. With our new son, Seth, we were venturing out into the grown-up world, where responsibilities beckoned. I used to think that working on a wildlife refuge in Montana banding trumpeter swans was the fulfillment of my dreams, but that was no longer an option. That just wouldn't pay the bills. I loved the outdoors and wild things, but a responsible family man must make responsible choices. Loving my family well meant provid-ing for their needs. We were young, healthy, and had our whole lives in front of us. Whatever we decided to do and wherever we decided to do it, was fine with us—as long as we were together. My wife and son were everything to me.

I've learned there is a clue to the secret of happiness and meaning in life and it is found in relationships. Shiny, new things are nice, but only if kept in the right perspective. Vacations are wonderful; mountain peaks and river-fed waterfalls are stunning; sunsets and sunrises are spectacular and can stir the human heart in ways that other stimuli cannot; but loved ones whom we have formed intimate relationships with are above all. Even a candy bar must take second fiddle here.

In his book *Can Man Live Without God*, Ravi Zacharias asserts, "There are four essential factors that give meaning to life: the *wonder* of childhood, the pursuit of *truth* in adolescence, the fulfillment of *love* in adult years, and finally *security* in our old age."[1] I think he's on to something here, and I highly recommend the book to anyone who wants to pursue a fruitful life. I'm not sure the stages of life and their key factors are as clear-cut as Dr. Zacharias makes them out to be on paper, however. I say this because I had transitioned to the adult *love* stage in life—my family was everything to me! Our second son, Trevor, was born three years after Seth. I loved Vicky, Seth, and Trevor more than anyone could possibly imagine. I am not gifted enough to describe this love with words. I was immersed in the fulfillment of love but had yet to satisfy my longing and desire to define and discover *truth*.

My first "professional" job after I graduated was working as a forester for a large electric utility company in Indiana. It was an entry-level position that was somewhat aligned with my training and college degree. It wasn't frontline, hands-on bird banding or collaring deer on a wildlife refuge as I had dreamed about, but this job meant that my family wasn't going to starve, and it afforded us a decent standard of living. There were many opportunities to grow in my position, plus about half of my time was spent out in the field away from the office and meetings. I was able to somewhat satisfy my longing for working outdoors in nature while learning and growing exponentially in my ability to work with all types of coworkers and customers.

I stayed with this job for nearly seven years before taking a similar position with a company in Wisconsin that had more opportunity for growth and the chance to run my own program. The new job brought with it the challenges of moving my family to a different state, adapting to a different work environment and culture, learning to fit in with new coworkers, and all the unexpected little things that go with any move or new position. During my twelve-plus years with this company, I had the opportunity to work as a staff professional, a first-line supervisor, and eventually a mid-level manager. Again, I took advantage of all the opportunities that were placed before me to grow as a professional, as a manager, and as a leader. I worked with a tremendous group of people, learned a lot, and continued to be blessed to spend at least a portion of my work week outdoors and away from the office and meetings.

Since I was a uniquely trained vegetation management professional working in a company made up of primarily engineers and accountants, all the higher-ups in management let me do my own thing. Nobody was looking over my shoulder micromanaging my department the way I heard so many others complain about. I really had the ideal job. My director and vice president at the time even talked to me about a promotion higher up the corporate ladder, but I preferred to stay connected to real people. By real people, I mean people who actually do real, meaningful work for a living.

In the corporate world, the further removed you are from real people who do real work, the more likely you are to be disappointed and frustrated with the folks you work with. I don't mean this to sound like an indictment on any individuals from my past or from upper management as a whole; no, no, one thousand times no! It's simply a fact of life. Some folks are great coworkers while some are not; that's the human condition. I have personally known executives who are tremendous people, people who make great contributions in the lives of those whom they are privileged to lead and serve. I have also known many frontline employees who have done the very same. It has simply been my experience that the further you get away from people who do real, meaningful work for a living, the less rewarding your work will be.

Whether we know it or not, or whether we consciously think about it or not, we all seek meaning and purpose in life. Anyone's life would seem unsatisfying and banal without purpose and meaning. The relationships that we form and maintain are key components that contribute to a fruitful and meaningful life. Truth, and how we define it, is also an essential element of a purpose-driven life.

6

LEARNING AS A PARENT

Early on in my professional career I made a strategic and intentional decision to make certain my vocation did not get in the way of loving my wife and raising my sons. I didn't make that decision based on a book I read or some marriage and family counseling session. I made it from observing the breakdowns and struggles of the men around me at work when they pursued money and position rather than spending time at home with their families. Could you really do both—climb the corporate ladder and have a strong family? That would be the ultimate achievement of the American dream, would it not? I didn't want to end up divorced and have my children divide their time between their parents. I was only in my early thirties at the time, and I had never seen anyone achieve financial success *and* have a great marriage and be an ideal father. I began to view it as an either/or situation—either I would pursue vocational success, or I would focus on being a good husband and father. I chose the latter of the two.

Just to be clear, I was an extremely motivated young man who wanted the best for my family. And yes, it was important that "the best for my family" included not wanting for necessities and being able to afford to live comfortably wherever we chose. I still wanted to provide well for us. I wanted to hold my head high while others observed and said, "Wow, he looks to be a great husband and father." I also wanted to be able to walk into any convenience store at any time and gaze across the candy counter and select my favorite candy bar. I wanted my version of the American dream as much as anyone, and that's how I chose to define it.

When I look back over the years Vicky and I spent raising our children, I think of extremely enjoyable, influential, and fruitful times—and years that flew by at supersonic speed. "Wow!" is the best way to express it! Of course, parenting continues as long as we are alive, but our years of daily, active parenting were very special indeed. There is no greater privilege than to pour into, care for, love on, laugh with, cry with, and lead your children as you prepare them to be happy, healthy, successful adults. We understood then, just as much as we do today, that having healthy children is indeed no small thing.

Being that we had two boys—Seth and Trevor—that made Vicky the only female in a house of three males, so she had to adjust a bit. But I think she loved every minute of it. On second thought, I don't *think* she loved it, I *know* she loved it! Being a mother of two boys and doing primarily boy-type activities—like youth sports and hiking—didn't disappoint her in the least. She loved all of us with all of her heart, and we knew it.

I think it is natural, to some degree, for young boys to like the things their fathers like. That's not always the case, but that was the case for both of my sons. Early on, they took a liking to basketball. They liked playing all sports in all seasons, but basketball was their favorite. Since they were both born and raised their first few years in Indiana, they received a natural indoctrination into youth basketball at a very early age. But when we moved to Oregon, Wisconsin, and discovered there was no youth basketball, what could I do but organize and form one in our local community? That probably sounds like no big deal, but the first year alone we had forty teams—second through sixth grade—sign up to participate in the very first Oregon Youth Basketball League, which is still active today. Holy smokes, what had I done?! To say that my life was too busy would be a gross understatement. I had basically added another full-time job onto an already full-time vocational job.

During the formation of the youth basketball league, I first had to meet with school administrators, the principals of three schools, and the head maintenance person at each school in order to get approval to use their facilities and to install adjustable-height basketball hoops. I also had to lead fundraising events, recruit forty volunteer basketball coaches, arrange for practice times, find game referees, and develop game schedules for twenty games to be held each Saturday in three local gymnasiums. And here's the kicker: I did it all before we had email and cell phones. Whew! Does that sound simply crazy? It was! But that's what I wanted to do, not only for my boys, but also for the other 398 local boys and girls who wanted to play basketball at a young age.

I was the commissioner for our youth basketball league for seven years. Where I found the time and energy to pull it off, I'll never know. When I look back on those days, our family enjoyed each and every practice night and all the game days. As the boys grew older, they were involved with their school teams and local summer leagues, but we didn't participate in any of the craziness of regional or out-of-state traveling teams. Seth and Trevor also wanted to participate in other seasonal sports and activities, so we didn't go overboard with any one thing. We also set aside time for normal outings, visits with out-of-state family, and vacations. My sons and I would also escape to central Wisconsin each year during the last week of October for our annual four-day camping and grouse hunting trip.

I was glad Seth and Trevor developed a fondness for being in nature like I had. It was a pleasure watching them grow up and seeing their appetite for the outdoors mature with age. Sitting around evening campfires in the chilly October air was special for each of us as we talked about how many birds we had flushed and missed during the day and what catches the next day might bring. We also talked and laughed about a lot of topics unrelated to hunting or camping. We developed lifelong bonds and created memories that have endured a lifetime. We were growing in our love for one another and didn't even know it at the time. We were also learning how to keep our toes warm when the temperature dropped into the teens at night.

My sons and I recently hiked and camped in the Bighorn Mountains of Wyoming, and we had a great time together, but it did not compare to the sweetness of fellowship experienced at our annual October camping trips in central Wisconsin. I don't know why those outings were so special, but they were. They were so very special.

If I could reflect on one great lesson I learned from those years, it would be this: if you want to be the ideal father, have more than two children. (Vicky and I had plans to have more than two, but as it turns out, she just wasn't able.) I know this must sound like strange advice. There are countless books on parenting written by highly credentialed professionals who've drawn from their own experience, education, and training on how to be a great parent. And I bet there aren't many (or even one) who would suggest such a drastic measure as having more children. There's probably no reasonable or scientific basis for such an assertion on my part, but hear me out: there was simply too much focus and energy from me for only two children to bear.

I was driven to be the perfect father. Whatever that meant exactly or whatever that looked like, I really didn't know—I was like a bird learning on the fly. But I do know I loved my boys with all of my heart, and I wanted the very best for them. Looking back, I feel as though I learned far more from my children than I ever taught them. By that I mean I learned from the process of being a parent and all the decisions you have to make—decisions that would shape their little hearts and minds as they grew up to be men. It was during this season of life that I first sensed the presence of genuine agape love. There was a tension that existed between loving well and the misdirected obsession to be the perfect father. On one hand, this new love called me to invest and sacrifice mightily for my children, but the pride of the flesh, at times, got in the way.

Vicky and I weren't the kind of parents who bought our children everything they wanted or who made sure they went to

Disney World. We didn't spoil them with excess stuff; we spoiled them with our time and attention. I wanted to be the perfect father, but my children didn't want a perfect father. They just wanted one who was present and who loved them, taught them, and cared for them.

I made the mistake of assuming that, since my father had zero time to spend with me, a child who had a father involved in his or her life would be better off. While that is generally true for most children, too much time and attention wasn't the perfect recipe either. As is usually the case, misdirected loves are exactly that—misdirected.

Upon reflection, I can honestly say I don't think there was a specific behavior or action on my part that proved damaging to my children. As adults, they've never come forth with any particular memory they wished was not part of their upbringing or a particular characteristic I had that bothered them. But I think I gave them too much hands-on attention. There was just too much of me. They've never said this to me directly, but I believe it to be so. In retrospect, I should have directed more time and energy into being a better husband to Vicky. I should have redirected more of my energy toward being a more loving son or brother or friend or community member or leader at church. While I think it's important to be involved, I've learned it's not necessary to be involved in *every* detail of a child's life. Balance is key. Children need space to think and grow for themselves and just be kids. So I think that if Vicky and I had more children, there would have been less of me to spread around and more time and space for them to grow.

Today Vicky and I are blessed to have a few young families in our lives who have many children. When we visit them, or when they come over to our home, I am reminded of how children are able to entertain and occupy themselves. Oh, how busy these young families are! Their houses are full of life, and there's only so much of Mom or Dad to spread around, but each child gets just the right amount of individual attention. Each of them knows they are loved and well cared for even as they compete with one another for more of Mom and more of Dad.

We seldom get do-overs in life, so we must dust ourselves off, learn from our experiences, and move on. We don't always have control over everything that happens in our lives, and that's most likely for our own good. Can you imagine the burden of carrying the control over all of your circumstances? That would simply be too much to bear.

As I mentioned earlier, the years we spent raising our children went by at warp speed. There were no "terrible twos," nor were there any seasons of extended illness that required an extra measure of parental endurance. Our youngest son did have allergies, asthma, and associated respiratory issues, plus a broken bone or sprained ankle here and there, but other than that, life was good. We truly enjoyed each season with them, and we wouldn't trade our experiences for anything.

Since we had boys, and boys sometimes wait until the ages of, say, seventeen to twenty-two before they do things that cause their parents great angst, we managed to put a lot of good years under our belts before facing any serious trials. But part of being a parent is facing hardship head-on and doing the best you can to fight through it together. We had some undesirable experiences in the young adult stages, but we came out the other end better for it. Again, I learned more from parenting my children than they ever learned from me.

I recall a telephone conversation I had with my mother around the time one of our adult sons was living dangerously and doing some really stupid things. The consequences of his behavior were sleepless nights and anxiety for Vicky and me. Perhaps that was one of his motives—I'm not sure. If it was, it worked! We were more than concerned, and we longed for his return to safer and more purposeful living. During this season, I couldn't help but think of the magnitude of sorrow and grief that all moms and dads face with their young adult children. There must have been countless late-night conversations that were muttered in my parent's tiny bedroom just off the kitchen in our small farmhouse as one child after the other made poor or questionable decisions that were contrary to how they had been taught and raised.

After giving my mom a brief synopsis of what was going on, I asked her to forgive me for any grief and gray hair I had caused her so many years earlier with my own poor decisions and actions growing up. Mom paused, thanked me for my heartfelt concern, and then replied, "I hear what you're saying Greg, I really do. But at my age, I don't remember any of that grief or the negative things you are speaking of. I only remember the good things." Oh, how I longed for that kind of parental maturity.

When it comes to being a parent, we do the best we can and

learn along the way. We are seldom equipped to make all the right moves and make all the right decisions, but we grow exponentially in the process. We have reached a place of parental maturity when we can reflect back and only remember the good things. I have learned far more from my children than they will ever learn from me.

7

PROCESSING THE DEATHS

OF LOVED ONES

I was forty-two years old, married to a beautiful woman who was my best friend, and had two healthy sons whom I loved very much. I lived in an extremely nice house in a great neighborhood, and I had a good job earning an above-average salary. I was healthy, and still I found myself saying, "There has to be more to life than this." I had achieved a portion of the great American dream, and it was not delivering what I thought it had promised. Vicky and I were no happier at that time than when we were first married and living in a two-bedroom, furnished apartment for $140 a month. We had more stuff and nicer stuff, plus more insurance policies to protect us in case our stuff was lost, stolen, or damaged, but we were no happier. Although I didn't hate my job by any means, I found that I usually worked sixty hours a week and often more. Was there any conceivable chance that I was going to continue to do this for the next twenty years? There had to be more to life than this, right? Whatever God had in mind for us at the beginning of the ages, I wasn't convinced it was this. There had to be a greater purpose in life. Why was I not content when, clearly, things weren't that bad and could be a whole lot worse? All my life I had witnessed an uncommon, almost supernatural contentment in my mother, yet I exhibited none of that.

I think my season of discontent started in earnest a few years earlier while I participated in a mid-management seminar/retreat with my coworkers. I had already been introduced to Stephen Covey's *The 7 Habits of Highly Effective People*, along with other readings and teachings that make even a good leader a better leader in the workplace. It was during that seminar that I received the news my father had a serious heart attack and was lying in a room at St. Vincent's hospital in Indianapolis, Indiana. It was serious enough that my brothers and sisters, who were living in California at the time, were headed to Indiana to be at his side. I packed my bags and left the resort in Wisconsin and drove straight to Indianapolis, where I met up with my mother and several of my siblings.

The next morning, I was able to visit with my father at his bedside, along with my mother and sister Ronda. With a surprised look on his face, Dad asked me, "Greg what are you doing here? Did you drive all the way from Wisconsin just to see me?" He was holding back tears as he must have realized things were pretty serious if all of his children were beginning to gather at the hospital. It was during this visit in his room when the cardiologist came in to see Dad and provide the diagnosis and recommendation of heart surgery. Immediately upon hearing the words from the doctor, Dad looked up at him and spoke solemnly with a quivering lip, "You mean open heart surgery, right?" That was the first and only time I ever witnessed my father cry as tears rolled down his cheeks, off the bottom of his chin, and on to the bed linens. We were at his side comforting him, and it wasn't long until he came to grips with the situation and developed a mindset of, "Okay, if that's what it takes, then I'm ready for surgery."

It was an extraordinary morning in the hospital, as all of my siblings and other relatives came to check in on him, wish him encouragement, and show him love. But within just a few short hours after speaking with the cardiologist, we heard a code blue announced over the hospital intercom, and many folks dressed in medical gowns rushed into his room, where they tried to revive him. He died with my mother, his wife of fifty-four years, at his side. It was March 5, 1993.

My father's death was a very significant event, to say the least. Up until that point in time, I had never experienced the death of an immediate family member, so this was the first. Those of you who have gone through this know exactly what I felt like, whereas those of you who haven't just don't know what you don't know. It's impossible to put all the emotions into words; it is simply something that is experienced deep within the mind, body, spirit, and soul. When I left the hospital that day, I followed my brother Harold to his home nearby, where we sat together and had a debriefing of what had just happened. We needed to wrap our minds around all that had transpired and what that would mean for our mother in the coming days.

Later that day, I left Harold's house and headed east on I-70 from Indianapolis toward the family farm where I grew up. In hindsight, I should not have been driving at all. One moment I was thinking clearly and driving the posted speed limit, then suddenly

I would find myself driving only 35 mph while my mind wandered all over the place and cars and semitrucks whizzed by. The only thing I remember about that drive was that I couldn't remember actually making the trip. I was in a thick fog with thoughts that were not of this world, and I have no idea how I arrived at the family farm safely.

Life had changed in an instant. Life would never again be the same. Each of my siblings experienced the loss differently, of course, since we all had uniquely different relationships with Dad. Since I was a middle child, and since I had moved away from home when I was eighteen years old, I didn't really have an intimate relationship with my father. There was only so much of Dad to go around, and he had a lot of people and responsibilities competing for his time. So why in the world did his death impact my inner being so greatly? We didn't have any unresolved issues to work out like the ones you see played out in movies or novels. Maybe it was the impact I thought his death would have on Mother's life. Would she continue to live on the farm, or would she move to town? Would her faith in God be enough to get her through this ordeal or would she succumb to the pangs of grief and wither away to nothing, a mere shadow of her previous self? Perhaps it was the fear of the unknown in the days to come that made such an unsettling change so deep down in my inner being.

I recall a conversation I had with my neighbor John after returning home to Wisconsin following Dad's funeral. He was able to offer words of encouragement and comfort—he lost his father a few years earlier. He also offered this nugget of wisdom to me: "You don't really grow up until your father is gone." Hmmm, maybe I had some growing up yet to do.

Life returned to somewhat normal rhythms following my father's passing, but I already knew that life would never be the same. One of the things that changed was a reconnection with my adult siblings. Just as a reminder, I had twelve brothers and sisters living in California, Ohio, and Indiana, while Vicky and I made our home in Wisconsin. We were spread out and, quite naturally, engaged in raising our own families and pursuing our own vocations. In large families, it is normal for closeness to develop in groups of similar ages or interests. That was certainly the case with Randy and me, but Harold was my closest brother during this particular time of healing. I'm not sure how or why this came to be; perhaps it was through his affection for my children. Harold certainly loved my sons. He spoiled them at every opportunity by buying them the most popular Jordan basketball shoes, sports-related attire, or just gifting them special things he knew they'd like.

After we moved to Wisconsin, my other siblings in the Midwest would come now and then for a visit, but those visits soon faded away, and the only regular visiting relatives were my sister Ronda, Vicky's sister Karen, and my brother Harold. Harold was self-employed as a hair stylist, and he worked a lot of hours as a result of the choice to own a salon. But despite the busyness in his life, he always made time to come to Wisconsin for a few days at a time to do life alongside us. Following Dad's passing, the visits were even more special, it seemed. Our conversations were more meaningful and the fellowship sweeter. But Harold was still Harold, and he would aggravate the dickens out of me from time to time, just like brothers often do.

Harold loved to buy my children things, sometimes out of love, but often just to drive me nuts. Vicky and I sat down with him time and time again to explain how much we appreciated his relationship with our boys, but spoiling them with excess wasn't our idea of what's best for our children. He heard us, but he would continue his obsessive behavior simply out of spite and to get a rise from his younger, Mr. Perfectionist brother. Vicky could overlook it, but I struggled with it and Harold knew it, so he had the upper hand and was crowned the winner of this strange, affectionate battle of who could aggravate the other more. We all loved Harold immensely, despite Harold being Harold. But, oh, how I wanted to strangle him at times!

During the weeks and months following Dad's passing, my relationship with Harold grew much deeper. We had been close for years, but now we were really learning to love one another. It was during this time that Harold began to notice the return of a cancerous growth on his foot. The growth had been treated by an oncologist years prior, but then it reappeared and required attention. The damage resulted from when the top of his foot had been severely sunburned during a time of respite on a beach while serving in Vietnam. Harold recalled that he had fallen asleep while sunbathing but woke up to the surprise of being overcooked. The spot had been on his foot for some time and it looked troublesome. He had it checked, and it turned out to be melanoma.

In October, my sister Linda drove Harold to our house to spend a week enjoying the family and the burst of vibrant, autumn colors. He could no longer drive himself, as the cancer on his foot, and now leg, had grown aggressively out of control. He had already moved out of his home in Indianapolis and was being cared for by Mom and our siblings at the farm. He had good days and bad days. Since he was feeling up to a trip, he asked Linda to drive him to our house for a visit. We were glad to see them both—all of us were anxiously looking forward to our visit. Linda didn't stay long, but she explained Harold's medical needs and medications to us before she headed back. It was a Saturday when they arrived, and I was to take Harold back home the following weekend.

The next day, we loaded up the minivan and headed up to Devil's Lake State Park for a picnic in the spectacular outdoors. We were blessed with a warm, sunny but breezy day, and we all had a great time enjoying one another and the time that had been given to us. Harold's face lit up as he watched Seth, Trevor, and me toss the football around while the orange, red, and yellow sugar maple leaves fell softly to the ground. Harold sat contently with a blanket wrapped around his legs as he ran his fingers through his hair. He'd clasp his fingers together momentarily to pull out a handful of hair from his scalp. He would then slowly open his hand and the gentle breeze would lift the hair from his fingers and spread it across the newly fallen leaves. The chemo and radiation were taking a toll on my beloved brother.

I went to work on Monday morning and the boys went off to school. Vicky stayed home to visit with and look after Harold, but this would not be the normal, fun-loving visit she'd grown accustomed to—he was struggling with pain. In fact, he was taking narcotics about three times the normal level and would run out of medication well before returning home the following weekend. He could no longer get comfortable no matter what he tried. He could not get comfortable in our minivan either, as the suspension was too stiff, and this made it painful for him to ride in the vehicle.

Since we knew we had to get him back to Indiana soon, I rented a Lincoln Continental luxury car and made a makeshift bed in the backseat for him to lie down as we traveled. This proved to be far more comfortable. We rode for eight hours together—just Harold and me—back to Mom's house. There was silence, there were conversations interrupted by screams of pain, there was singing, and there were oh, so many tears that flowed down each of our faces. I tried everything I knew to comfort him, but with little success. He was simply in a different place than I was, and I knew it. It was a long, long drive back home to Indiana that night.

When we finally arrived at the farm, Harold's anxiety had lessened, and he was clearly relieved to be back. Mom and my sisters made him a quasi-home-bed-nursing station in the living room where they could care for him. He stayed there about a week, then moved to my sister Betty's house, where she would be his primary caregiver along with a lot of help from her daughters, sisters, and brothers. Even though everyone had full-time jobs and families of their own to tend to, they cheerfully and willingly sacrificed together to make it work.

Three weeks later, he breathed his last breath. Harold died exactly six months to the day after Dad had passed. My favorite brother was gone. Harold was gone.

During the days leading up to Harold's passing, I struggled with anxiety, but I didn't know it. That may sound a little confusing, but let me explain. Vicky and I had just stepped out of a movie theater one evening when I experienced severe chest pains. We thought I was having a heart attack, so Vicky immediately drove me to the emergency room, where I went through all sorts of tests to see if, indeed, a relatively healthy and athletic-looking thirty-eight-year-old was actually ready to kick the bucket. As it turns out, I wasn't having a heart attack, so I was sent home with instructions to see my regular doctor as soon as possible. During the follow-up appointment, my doctor kept asking questions like, "Are you experiencing extra stress at work? Are things messy at home?" I wasn't sure where he was headed until I mentioned Harold's illness. He then explained that I might be expressing symptoms of stress associated with anxiety from my brother's condition. He suggested I continue wearing the heart monitor I was given just in case I had a condition that wasn't discovered while at the hospital.

I stood gazing at the stars on that clear and cool November night prior to Harold's funeral. I was standing motionless in the barn lot of the Indiana family farm beside the shed where we used to play basketball for countless hours on end. I looked to the heavens for something, but I wasn't sure what. I reached down to see if my heart monitor was still in place and went back to gazing at the night sky. It was just me alone with my thoughts, trying to process all that had happened that year. Maybe I needed to be alone to let my emotions swirl about, or perhaps God was inviting me to draw closer to Him or lean into Him in a brand-new way. My upward gaze soon blurred with tears. They were warm tears that flowed down my cheeks and dripped off my face that evening. They were tears of mercy and tears of comfort. They were necessary tears.

There are times in life when we are alone—just us and our Creator. It is often after a huge gash has been ripped through our heart that we feel especially hopeless and vulnerable. Our tears testify to this. It is during these moments that we either draw nearer to God for comfort or we push Him further out of the picture. What are we to do with this hole that dwells within us?

8

A HOLY DISCONTENTMENT

Life after Harold's death continued to press a sense of discontentment upon me. I discovered that having a nice family, a good job, a comfortable house—all the things that make up the American dream—had not really satisfied the longing I had for a happier, more fulfilling life. I even had some real "highs" in my mix of experiences, such as vacations to Rocky Mountain National Park, going to an NCAA Final Four basketball game in New Orleans, and touring Washington, DC. They were amazing, but not amazing enough to bring me the contentment I desired. Two years prior to the deaths of Dad and Harold, I had begun my search for greater meaning in life. I had purchased the self-help books that were popular at the time, listened to numerous tapes on the philosophy of world religions that addressed the big questions in life, and even started reading the Bible. I also read the book *Man's Search for Meaning* by Viktor Frankl.

This book details the life of a professional psychologist as he endured Nazi death camps during World War II. Frankl explored the quest of finding ultimate meaning in life and how affliction and suffering aided in this discovery. He wrote that excruciating living conditions and lack of freedom can lead a man to discern the true, inner longings of his heart and mind. And here I sat in the middle of wonderful living conditions with all the freedoms in the world, yet I was distraught and searching for something more. If Frankl would have had an opportunity to trade places with me, he likely would have done so in an instant, and in the process, shed tears of thanksgiving and joy. Regardless of circumstance, perhaps we are all wired to discover this on our own? After twice experiencing grief and loss within a six-month period, I began to change.

Drastic changes in one's life often follow the death of a loved one. This was not only so in my life, but I have frequently observed it in the lives of my friends and family members. In loss, we have an opportunity to draw closer to God in a brand-new way. However, some people choose the opposite and get mad at God and push Him further out of their lives. Regardless of what we do, it's not life as it was—change results from knowing we'll be separated from a loved one for the rest of our life.

By this time, half of my life was now in the rearview mirror, and my search for greater meaning and purpose had been going on for about six years. I had come to the realization that I could no longer continue down the same "typical" path I had been on. One of the changes I knew I had to make was to leave my corporate job to get away from the routine of life for a while. I needed time to think with a clear, clutter-free mind. The French mathematician and philosopher Blaise Pascal once wrote in his composition *Pensées*, "The sole cause of man's unhappiness is that he does not know how to stay quietly in his room."[2]

What he was saying is, we are afraid to be alone with our thoughts. We constantly surround ourselves with trendy diversions to distract us from the truly important things in life, such as purpose, meaning, and mission. And that's precisely what I needed to do—be still and quiet enough to hear myself think. I needed to disengage. I needed to get alone with the God who created me so I could ponder what the remainder of my life should look like. Socrates once wrote, "The unexamined life is not worth living." Above all else, I did not want to waste the rest of my life—I wanted one that was worth living.

Pascal's writings are very thought-provoking, to say the least, and they invite readers to think more seriously and deeply than most authors challenge you to do. He went on to write,

> When I consider the brief span of my life absorbed into the eternity which comes before and after—as a remembrance of a guest that tarrieth but a day—the small space I occupy and which I see swallowed up in the infinite immensity of spaces which I know nothing and which know nothing of me, I take fright and am amazed to see myself here rather than there: there is no reason for me to be here rather than there, now rather than then. Who put me here? By whose command and act were this time and place allotted to me? . . . Anyone with only a week to live will not find it in his interest to believe that all of this is a matter of chance.[3]

Life and how we choose to live it is the very essence of what matters most. To take life lightly and to live it without a purpose is not only silly, but foolish. We must indeed have answers to the questions concerning the origin of life and the purpose it holds.

If we fail to live in view of the answers, we end up wasting our life compared to what it could be otherwise.

Pascal, a great thinker, had indeed given another thinker, me, a lot to think about. This brilliant man reasoned that life makes absolutely no sense unless God is in the picture. Things just didn't come about by chance. Pascal wasn't always of that mindset, but his searching and reasoning brought him to that conclusion. He asserts, "There are only three sorts of people: (1) those who have found God and serve him; (2) those who are busy seeking him and have not found him; and (3) those who live without either seeking or finding him. The first are reasonable and happy, the last are foolish and unhappy, those in the middle are unhappy and reasonable."[4]

Peter Kreeft, professor of philosophy at Boston College, offers this commentary about the three sorts of people in his book *Christianity for Modern Pagans*:

> Group 1 are believers in God. They are reasonable because they seek and are happy because they have found. Group 2 are unhappy atheists and agnostics. They are reasonable because they seek and are unhappy because they have not yet found. Group 3 are the contented atheists. They are unreasonable, foolish, and spiritually insane, because they do not even seek the truth; they are unhappy (forever) because they do not find God. The great divide, the eternal divide, is not between theists and atheists, or between happiness and unhappiness, but between seekers and non-seekers of the Truth (God is Truth).[5]

Pascal's reasoning led him to the promise that Jesus made in Matthew 7:7–8: "Ask, and it will be given to you; seek, and you will find; knock, and it will be opened to you. For everyone who asks receives, and the one who seeks finds, and to the one who knocks it will be opened." I was hoping this promise was indeed true.

I was beginning to realize I was searching for a life different from the one I had, but I didn't know what that life looked like or what influence God might have on that life. I was not content.

My mother possessed an extraordinary contentment. I respected and admired her greatly for displaying that virtue. But I've heard there is such a thing as holy discontentment. Its Author is God. I was beginning to discover what holy discontentment was all about.

9

RETREAT TO THE MOUNTAINS

Four months after Harold died, Vicky and I bought forty acres of land that was located about ten miles from our existing residence. We had been thinking about it for a while—getting a place in the country where we could get back to our rural upbringing. The deaths of my dad and brother moved this priority up on our list far enough that we actually made it happen. We showed up at a public auction on that frigid, late winter morning and became the owners of a forty-acre rolling parcel of land along Smith Road in Brooklyn Township. We could hardly believe it. We had land!

We were giddy with our new acquisition. No two people in southern Wisconsin could have been more on fire with enthusiasm than we were on that day. We were ecstatic as we parked our car along Smith Road and hiked back along the edge of the field through thigh-deep snow toward our small woodlot.

Our dream of starting a Christmas tree farm was turning into a reality. I had always longed to create, cultivate, tend to, and grow things outdoors away from computer screens, frustrated coworkers, and meetings. I believe there is a shared, built-in unction among most men—and even some women—to accomplish real work with their own hands or machinery and to see tangible results when they are done. Men who love the outdoors want to build things, cut down dead trees with a chainsaw, and burn a pile of brush. I was now one of those fortunate guys who would get to do just that. Nine years from that day, we would provide our very first Christmas tree to our very first customer. It was all so exciting—I wondered what else God had in store.

Just a few years after purchasing our land, I found myself standing in a newly planted field of balsam firs and talking with God. It was the day I decided to finally leave my corporate job and start anew. I told Him, "I believe You have a different view of what life should look like here on earth. Help me place my trust in You by faith. If I leave this good job and comfortable lifestyle, will You do Your part by providing for our needs? If I do my part, I expect You to do Your part, okay? Please don't let me down—this is new territory for me. I'm used to taking care of everything myself, but something inside of me is urging me to change and turn my plans over to You. Help me not waste the rest of the precious life You have given to me. I have no idea what the next chapter looks like, but I'm sure that You have a desire to be a bigger part of it, right?"

So, I did it! I actually quit my job without lining up another job to transition into. Who does that, anyway? Some people do, but not folks who are wrapped like me. I'm a responsible family man who doesn't have a slacker bone in his body. I was both excited and a little scared. I had just left a job that provided us a very comfortable lifestyle. My plan was to take a minimum of six months away from income-earning work so I could be free to get alone with my thoughts and discern what I'd do with the remainder of life I had left. I was on a mission. Perhaps you've noticed the abundance of "I" and "My" in the last few paragraphs and have wondered, *What did Vicky have to say about him quitting his job and doing nothing for six months? Why didn't he include her in any of "his plans?"* Well, not to worry, Vicky and I were of one accord. She was fully behind the decision—and she thought that surely, I'd be more pleasant to live with in my new, decluttered life.

My soul is nourished in the great outdoors. In America, I don't think there's a grander place to experience the splendor of nature and to cleanse the mind than in the mountains of the West. So, soon after leaving my job, I headed out west with Seth. He spent the first ten days or so with me as I began my soul-searching retreat, but even he had to get back to normal life responsibilities. The time we had together was incredibly special. He listened while I explained what I had been going through, and I grew to know him better as well. We also shared lots of laughs and stories, made some memories at stops along the way, and experienced the splendor of God's creation. Oh, and we also hiked down into and back out of the Grand Canyon. Yes, you read that correctly—we hiked the Grand Canyon. To anyone who is physically able and has an attraction to the natural created order of things, I highly recommend it.

I believe God made the canyon lands of southern Utah in order to keep the less spectacular places in their proper perspective. There are enormous towers, arches, buttes, balanced rocks, and plateaus that continuously change their appearance and color as the sun rises over the sky. The red sandstone faces light up like giant lanterns when they intercept the morning's first rays of sunlight. If I were a talented writer, I would continue to write eloquently of the splendor of this landscape, but I'm not. It's hard to put into words, so I strongly encourage you to see it for yourself. It's my belief that a lot of folks who visit the mountains and canyons in the West are looking for something deep within, whether they realize it or not. It's true, some people just want to escape their routine for a long weekend or for a few days away to enjoy the fresh air and the beauty that is on display before them. But most go to the mountains not simply to discover what's around the corner bolder or down the canyon wall or what lies on the other side of the saddleback, but also to dream something greater about themselves and life itself. There is a closer connection with the God who created it all, whether they know it or not.

I spent the entire month of June out west decluttering. I had time to reflect on the joys and challenges of marriage; what it would look like to be a better father to my sons from this point forward; how I could be a more loving husband; how I might steward the land I had been granted; what my vocational options were; and how would I actually pay the bills moving forward. The Christmas tree farm was small and would only provide a part-time income for us in the future. It was an excellent adventure and retreat, but only the beginning of a process that I hoped would lead to a more fruitful and meaningful life. But true to form, even the most well intended vacations, or in this case, an intentional retreat, must come to an end. I recorded this entry in my journal near the end of my trip: "I would rather be home now." I guess you can only fill your senses with so much until the newness wears off and home becomes even more attractive than the grandest of national parks, forests, or wilderness areas. I wrote on, "Home is where I'd rather be right now, as it is a beautiful place to be as well." I took one last look at the Wyoming campground where I was staying, packed up my belongings, and began to head east.

Near the end of my journey toward home, I stopped at a gas station convenience store along I-90/94 in western Wisconsin, just a couple of hours from home, to use the restroom and to buy a pack of gum. On this beautiful, sunny morning, I found myself in line behind a four-year-old blond-haired boy named Nathan. He was full of energy, shuffling back and forth on his knees in front of the candy rack, captivated by all the selections on display. The emotions and excitement exhibited by this youngster rivaled what you would expect to see on Christmas morning. While his mother waited patiently in line with him, I harkened back to my youth in front of the candy counter at Creager's 5 & 10 Cent Store. I knew what this little guy was going through, and he needed not to be rushed into making a decision he might later regret. I, along with everyone else standing in line, just needed to chill out and give Nathan some time to contemplate.

Nathan's mother shared with me that she stopped there to buy some Robitussin for Nathan's sister. As he continued to stare at all the candy, his mother said, "No, you're not getting any candy today, so don't even think about it." She didn't say it in a mean sort of way, just in a caring, motherly sort of way. I thought to myself, *Will this cycle ever end?* After a few more anxious seconds passed, his mom again stated, "Don't even think about it, Nathan." Despite his mother's refusal to buy him what he wanted, his determination to stare up and down the entire length of the fifteen-foot-long candy stand was quite impressive for me to witness, as a much older candy enthusiast. Nathan never wavered. I commented to his mother on Nathan's behalf, "Gee, it's really hard not to even *think* about it, Mom." She confessed, "Yes, I used to love these when I was a youngster as well." She was referring to the large package of grape flavored Fun Dips that Nathan was now nose-to-nose with. The Fun Dips were nestled in between the Nerds, the Gummi Savers, and the Snickers bars. I commented, "Well, I never had Fun Dips while I was growing up. Never even heard of them until Nathan pointed them out to me." The only candy I recognized from my childhood were the Snickers and Milky Way bars. Isn't it amazing how a candy counter can identify a specific generation of people?

During the nearly five-minute wait in line, Nathan's entire attention was on the candy in front of him, and nothing else. His hope was that his mother would have a change of heart and relent so a four-year-old boy could be as happy as he could be—even though the happiness would be short-lived. Nathan, his mother, and his sister left the store that day with only the Robitussin in hand. Although he was most likely disappointed, it was encouraging to see a young boy obey his mother without raising a fit or throwing a tantrum, as is so common these days. Nathan may have already been thinking of the silver lining in that morning's defeat—no candy today meant an increased chance of candy tomorrow or next week. Mothers can only hold out for so long before they eventually cave in to the cuteness and the longing to satisfy their children. Ahh, the anticipation of his next visit to the store with Mom was surely resting somewhere in Nathan's being as he left the store empty-handed that day.

I walked out behind this young family with a big grin on my face. I wasn't in a big hurry to pay for the chewing gum and get back on the road; I was beginning to slow down and experience the little things in life that bring a smile to your face and warm your heart. It had been a couple of months now since I had left my job, and I was already noticing the change in my demeanor and the positive effects of ridding myself of meaningless busyness. I'm certain the month I had just spent traveling out west contributed a whole lot to the new, improved version of myself as well. My mind was about as clutter-free as I could imagine. I was excited to see Vicky again, give her a long embrace, and tell her everything my heart and mind had experienced over the past weeks. I was eager to discover what God had in store for both of us as we set out to live the second half of our lives together.

10

THE AMERICAN DREAM

VS. GOD'S DREAM

I was well into my six-month cleansing phase of life when Vicky and I moved into our new home on the tree farm. I spent a good portion of my days working in the fields, working in the shed, or putting the finishing touches on the house and landscaping. There was plenty to keep me fruitful, and it was the kind of activity that renewed me. Vicky was struggling to keep a gift shop afloat in a nearby community, and the bills were surpassing our income. She loved doing what she was doing, and she loved the people part of the business, but she was spending a lot of hours barely making ends meet. In the meantime, we were living off a savings account that was dwindling with each passing month, but we were determined to be patient and stick with our plan.

Shortly after I had returned from out west, Vicky learned that her mother, Janet, was ill. Her parents had moved to South Carolina to be closer to their two daughters, who were living there at the time. Janet had broken her hip, and when the doctors performed surgery, they found cancer in the bone. After a battery of tests and fact finding, they found the cancer had developed in her kidney and spread throughout her body to the point where it was just a matter of time before she would succumb to the disease.

Vicky was able to spend the last three weeks of Janet's life by her side. She helped her die at home with dignity while surrounded by her husband and beloved daughters. Janet had placed her faith in Christ, so her passing was not a negative, miserable event. The whole family was able to witness her hope, and it lessened the painful sting of losing her. They were all with her when she breathed her last breath and the last bit of warmth from her body disappeared. Vicky's mother was gone.

Through the process of helping her mother die, Vicky was dramatically transformed and would never again be the same. Janet's death had brought new life—a changed life—to her. She returned to Wisconsin four days after the funeral, exhausted, thankful, and a new person. I praise God for His abounding mercy and grace through it all.

As I stated earlier, trials, struggles, and severe testing will cause us to either draw nearer to God or to push Him away. Vicky had experienced God's transforming power in a brand-new way that was good. Even though she had walked alongside me through my father and brother's passing, this was different. She had lost her mother, the one who gave birth to and nurtured her as a child; the one who went to her ballgames and school activities; the one who had always been there for her over the years. The mother who loved her dearly was now gone, and Vicky was not distraught or bitter—she was experiencing a peace that transcends natural understanding.

While Vicky was in South Carolina, I stepped in for her at the gift store. Since August was a slow month for store traffic, it afforded me the opportunity to read several good books written by critically thinking authors—I was still in my intentional season of reflection and discovery. I also devoured Scripture at an accelerated pace, and my years of searching were now producing the fruit of clarity. Vicky and I were changing, but how would this change translate into our lives moving forward?

One of my discoveries was that you cannot plan every little detail in life; you simply have to get out of bed each morning, step out, and live. I knew we both needed to keep living each new day with purpose, but at a pace and with an approach drastically different from what we had experienced most of our adult lives. When Vicky returned home, she decided to close her gift store.

The underlying conclusion I took away from life thus far and my season of meditation and discovery was this: life is no accident. My life didn't come into being by a hypothetical meeting of time plus matter plus chance. The Big Bang Theory plus the theory of evolution was not responsible for all of the intricacies in life, nor did they supply meaning. While the theory of evolution has merits at the micro level, it has no reasonable or logical explanation for the origin of life. God is the Author of life and the Creator of all things. He also formed me in His image for a purpose. That purpose is to glorify Him in all that I do and to enjoy Him forever. To glorify God and to enjoy Him forever is the reason any of us were created in the first place. This is in stark contrast to the American dream, where *we* are the center and substance of everything, not God.

I am formally educated in the life sciences and have read numerous books by authors who are PhDs. Many of them have been trained in biology, medicine, physics, mathematics, ecology, philosophy, and religion. As it turns out, many of those great thinkers came to the same conclusion I did: life only makes sense if God is at the center. Otherwise, it is meaningless and banal. Life lived with God at the center is like living a romance with the Author of life itself. Armed with this revelation and new worldview, I was now better prepared and at peace to live the second half of my life.

Winston Churchill once commented, "Men occasionally stumble over the truth, but most of them pick themselves up and hurry off as if nothing ever happened." I had been searching for truth most of my adult life; I wasn't about to ignore it and move on. Happiness in childhood was found in my favorite candy bar or a cold bottle of Nehi soda pop, but as an adult I wanted truth, authentic relationships, and deeper meaning to be at the center of my life. John Gardner, in his book *Self Renewal*, states, "If happiness could be found in material things and in being able to indulge yourself in things that you consider pleasurable, then we in America would be deliriously happy. We would be telling one another frequently of our unparalleled bliss, rather than trading tranquilizer prescriptions."[6] This appears to be in harmony with G. K. Chesterton's assertion that meaninglessness doesn't come from being weary of pain; meaninglessness comes from being weary of pleasure. More fun, more vacations, more toys, more pleasures, a bigger house, a better job, a new spouse, and the pursuit of them all of those things will not provide ultimate meaning or gratifying purpose in life. No, they will not provide happiness or sustaining joy! In our culture, we are weary of pleasure, not pain. And with each new generation, we seem to ratchet it up another notch. Oh my! We are entertaining ourselves into a stupor to the point where we actually believe this to be our primary pursuit in life. Pascal was right: we will do almost anything rather than sit quietly in our room, with no distractions, and be alone with our thoughts.

All of this self-examination and search for meaning led me to a crossroad. Whenever I turn on the television and scroll through shows and come across *The Shawshank Redemption*, I'll pause to watch at least a portion of it. The movie centers on the lives of a few key inmates as they endure long stays in prison. I especially like the scene where young Andy, portrayed by Tim Robbins, tells gray-haired Red, the prisoner portrayed by Morgan Freeman, "I guess it comes down to a simple choice, really. Get busy living or get busy dying." That simple statement is something that many of us should consider as we sit alone quietly in a room with no distractions—with only our thoughts. My crossroad led me to get busy living a purpose-driven, fruitful life.

Jesus taught His disciples in Matthew 6:19–21, "Do not lay up for yourselves treasures on earth, where moth and rust destroy and where thieves break in and steal, but lay up for yourselves treasures in heaven, where neither moth nor rust destroys and where thieves do not break in and steal. For where your treasure is, there your heart will be also." I believe this is very straightforward and requires little clarification. Wherever my treasure is, there my heart will be also. As long as I set apart God as my real treasure, my heart will be there with Him also. That is a wonderful promise, a promise too marvelous to pass up. Getting to know God intimately and to treasure Him above all earthly things was now the mission that shaped my new life.

It soon became clear to me what I'd do regarding my new vocation: I'd continue doing what I had been doing for the past twenty years. I decided to hang my own shingle and start a professional management services firm of one employee—me. I was very competent in my profession, and I'd developed a decent network of associates within the industry. I began to make contacts just to let prospective customers know that I was available and could help them if they needed assistance. I also mailed some letters and brochures with a similar message. I met a handful of potential customers for lunch dates, and that summed up my marketing plan. It wasn't long before I had my first request to complete a project for a company. It was a relatively small project, but a couple of months later that customer paid our very first invoice in full. Vicky and I once again had income!

A month or so later, I received another inquiry to assist a company with a workload assessment project. That fall and winter I performed four additional workload assessment projects for companies that had heard of the work I was doing. Those projects led to my firm being retained for managing ongoing work at those companies and one other nearby company. This surge in business also led me to hire an additional employee, then another employee, then another. Within the first year, I went from one employee to four employees, just like that. Our company was performing well, and our hands-on, low-tech marketing plan had paid off. Customers were quite satisfied with our services, and word spread about the work we were doing.

As of this writing, I've been in business for twenty-two years, and the income generated has comfortably provided for my family's needs. I've intentionally kept the company small, never having more than five employees and no website to maintain or to generate unwanted busyness. In my prior life, I had been overcommitted and too busy, so I was very careful not to let that happen again. Since those first few months after I formed the company, I have never made another sales call or sales visit. All of the jobs I've been privileged to take on have been the result of customers calling me and my team, not from any of us promoting or selling our services to customers. We have been blessed beyond measure, more than I could have ever hoped for or imagined.

I started this venture simply to provide income for our family and to enjoy the work that was placed before me. It was a vocation I knew how to do well, so I did it—mission accomplished. It was not my objective to become wealthy—also mission accomplished. But it was my objective to work and live at a much more relaxed pace and to have time and opportunity throughout the week to attend to more important matters in life—such as relationships with coworkers, friends, family, and loved ones. I've spent only about twenty hours per week on income-earning activities since I left my corporate job over twenty-two years ago. Yes, I've cheated the system! I recall vividly having that conversation with God in the field of balsam fir Christmas trees many years ago. I essentially asked Him to do His part if I did my part. He has been faithful on His end—He's provided for our every need and then some. In the process, I have been given a new way of life that enables me to do far more than just work and earn a living.

I really want to add something here that is a testament to the faithfulness of God. I don't mention it to boast in any way, because I know the nature of my own selfish heart, and I believe this will sound foreign and strange to many folks, but here are the facts: over the past two decades, it has been both a joy and a privilege for Vicky and me to gift 10–30 percent of our income each year to folks who are in financial need, to famine and disaster relief agencies, to global missions, and to our church. We have not done this out of a sense of obligation or duty, but because of an unmistakable desire in our hearts. It's been a process of growing in grace. When I left my corporate job, I was worried about how I would provide. I had never, ever imagined I would soon be giving away nearly one-third of my annual income. It probably sounds as though I am wealthy, so I can easily afford to give away money. No, that is not the case at all! Vicky and I have an average middle-class household income, but our desires and priorities have changed. Our lives are more fruitful than they've ever been—in our work, in our giving, and in our relationships. God has to be behind such a supernatural thing as this, because we have no other explanation for it.

Once you've crossed the Rubicon and have committed to growing in a relationship with God, there is a continual tension between your pursuit of the American dream versus God's dream for you. This tension is real, and it never completely goes away. God is faithful, however, and He wants the very best for you. If you fix your eyes on Him, He will transform your dreams into His.

11

FRUIT FROM TRIALS

S hortly after I launched my new business venture of professional services management, I was struck with just how much time I had wasted in my former corporate job just by attending meetings, along with other unfruitful activities. Wow! This new job required me to perform tasks that simply needed to be done for the success of the business and for the betterment of our customers and employees. The former job required me to attend a *lot* of meetings—staff meetings, employee informational meetings, project management meetings, training meetings, safety meetings, grievance hearings . . . I could go on and on. Of course, I had responsibilities of doing real work, but I had to fit it around all of the meetings—they seemed to always take priority. And it wasn't just the time spent in each actual meeting that was frustrating; it was also the time spent traveling to and from each meeting, which was often held in a satellite office location of the company. Meetings can certainly be helpful and are often necessary to accomplish an objective and maintain good communication, but I made sure there were a lot fewer meetings with my new business. I felt as if I had been untethered and granted extra hours to do the more fruitful work I enjoyed doing.

This was one of the most profound differences between my past job and my new one.

My new vocational life was certainly not without challenges. I don't want to leave you with the impression that I was living an endless fairy tale full of bliss. There were comforts associated with my prior job that I chose to leave behind. That's what made the decision difficult and not a simple slam dunk. Not only did I leave a good, consistent salary, I also walked away from a very plush employee benefits package. I now took on all the risks that my former employer had provided for all of those years. I now had the risk of uncertainty of income, financial liability for claims or litigation, the cost of pensions and benefits, concerns for employee safety, along with the mother lode of all burdens: insurance. Small businesses are simply strangled with the cost of insurance. There is general liability, professional liability, auto, errors and omissions, workers' compensation, health insurance, and probably other miscellaneous insurance I'm not remembering at the moment. All of these components added up to real, grown-up responsibilities that I would have never dreamed of as a youth on a small farm. I dreamed of my next candy bar back then, not running a business.

In spite of the new challenges in my business, life was better, and life was good. But I also developed another kind of challenge over time. Each morning as I rose out of bed, my body let me know I was no longer the youthful, healthy man I used to be. Around the time of my father's death, I was thirty-eight years old, and I began to experience excruciating lower back pain—at least, I thought it was excruciating at the time. Of course, I went to the doctor and did physical therapy, along with special exercises, but nothing improved. With time, the pain just became worse and more disruptive to my normal day-to-day activities. I really wanted my neurologist or orthopedic surgeon to say, "Greg, you have such-and-such wrong in your L4 and L5 joints. We can operate next week and make you as good as new." But I never heard those words. I simply had to deal with it.

I'm unsure of the source or cause of the initial lower back pain. I can only recall one significant blunt trauma that may have caused it. When Trevor was in elementary school, he took a pretty nasty tumble off his bicycle after getting tangled up with a friend's bicycle tire. Trevor came home limping, screaming, and crying. It appeared that Trevor was the victim of our family's very first broken arm, and he was in severe pain. Of course, I came to his rescue and applied a makeshift splint to stabilize his arm for the ride to the ER in Madison. Soon after we arrived and a physician examined his arm, an orthopedic surgeon was called in, and their advice was to forgo the risks of surgery and simply sedate Trevor to the point where he wouldn't feel anything, then quickly apply pressure to "snap" his bone back into place. Vicky and I asked the doctors to clarify for sure that our son would feel little or no pain, and they assured us that would be the case. Well, we were naïve and foolish young parents, so we put our trust solely in the doctor's opinion.

Again, being the almost perfect father who had come to the rescue of my son, I elected to stay at Trevor's side while the doctors did their bone setting. Vicky had already showed symptoms of sweat on her upper lip, limp legs, and a face as white as a sheet after seeing the bone sticking up in Trevor's forearm. She had nearly passed out a time or two, so I was going to be the hero and spare her any unnecessary discomfort and anguish.

Once the doctors administered the right amount of la-la-land medication to Trevor, they abruptly went about their business of setting the bone. I heard a haunting crunch followed by Trevor screaming at the top of his lungs, and Dad quickly passed out and slammed onto the hard tile floor. The only thing I remember about that fall was that my tailbone took 100 percent of the force of the fall. Ouch! When the ER nurse and Vicky finally woke me up, the doctors were done with Trevor and showed more concern with me than him. It was embarrassing and not what I had planned.

Whether that fall started my lower back pain or was just one of the factors that added to an issue that was already there, I do not know. I guess from a big-picture point of view, it doesn't matter a whole lot, but what does matter is how I responded and chose to live with it.

Over the years, the pain has only worsened—to the point of needing bilateral para-vertebrae facet joint injections every few months just to keep me upright and ambulatory. When the injections wear off, I eat Aleve tablets like they are Skittles until I get back to the pain management doctor to receive more injections. Recently, I had bilateral radio frequency ablation to "burn" or "kill" the nerve endings in specific joints in my lower back to help alleviate the discomfort. What I thought was excruciating pain twenty-four years earlier was nothing compared to what I experience today.

Fast forward to my aching process of getting out of bed . . . On top of all my usual back pain issues, I had also developed muscle spasm and cramping that would occur spontaneously all over my body. The neurologist referred to it as benign muscle fasciculation, or BFS. That's a mouthful, isn't it?! I'm not sure I even spelled it correctly. In layman's terms, this means ongoing muscle tremors—or fasciculations—in the large muscle groups of my body. If I were to sit in a bathtub of water while having an "episode," the muscle twitching would create waves on the surface of the water. The tremors aren't painful or disabling, they're just annoying. BFS is very similar to and often confused with Lou Gehrig's Disease (ALS), but thankfully, the neurologist assured me I did not have ALS. He told me BFS falls into the category of an *undefined* neuromuscular disorder. I think this is what a neurologist says when he knows his patient is in a lot of pain, but he doesn't know why.

Needless to say, the lower back pain combined with the debilitating muscle spasms and cramping, along with the annoying muscle fasciculations, were putting a damper on the lifestyle I thought I would live. I will be totally honest and confess, I even uttered the "why me?" question. In retrospect, I can see how selfish that utterance was.

Today, the muscle spasms and cramps still come and go, but I've learned they can be triggered by overworking a particular muscle group or by poor choices in diet or hydration—or sometimes for no reason at all. And, as I mentioned earlier, I've have learned to deal with the pain and accept it, but not without some help along the way . . .

Around ten years ago I met a fellow also named Greg, and we eventually became friends. He entered my life to help me learn how to cope with my pain and discomfort—not so much from the physical point, but mentally and emotionally. Chronic pain is the great equalizer, my friends. It has a way of sorting out things and reestablishing priorities. Nothing will gain your attention more or reshape your life as dramatically as severe physical pain. I've experienced how it has affected me, witnessed how my pain affects others around me, and noticed how another family member's pain affected the rest of us, most notably during the final months and weeks leading up to their death. I've come to learn that pain must be dealt with both physically *and* emotionally. Pain is a great teacher.

As Frankl said, there's no greater teacher than pain and the disability it causes. Books can provide insight, counselors can provide advice, and doctors will do their best, but they can all do only so much. Friends and loved ones are well-intentioned about how to help you, and some would even trade places with the one who is suffering if they could, but they can't.

God used my friend Greg to teach me about living with chronic discomfort day after day, year after year. He and I are the same age, and we have similar interests. He follows and roots for the Wisconsin Badgers basketball team, and I follow and root for the Purdue Boilermakers basketball team. He has a moose head hanging on his living room wall, and I have white-tailed deer antlers hanging in our Christmas tree shop. During my younger years I regularly jogged three to four times a week, and Greg has run four marathons. But Greg had a severe stroke fourteen years ago, and he hasn't been hunting or run a single step since.

By the time I met Greg, he was already homebound from the stroke. He no longer worked as a UPS driver, and he no longer had the ability to leave the house as he pleased. He has good days and he has not-so-good days. His wife must get him out of bed shortly after 6:00 a.m. each morning to bathe and dress him before she goes off to work a full-time job. If it's a warm day with a soft breeze and Greg is able to be outside, that's heaven on earth for him. He has taken a few spills while trying to walk from place to place over the years. As a consequence of the accidents, he has broken several bones and ended up in the hospital or nursing home for weeks or months at a time, but he bounces back. And aside from the physical struggles of navigating through his day, he must also somehow deal with the emotional struggles he faces. A prospect of recovery doesn't exist; his condition is permanent. It will be this way for the rest of his life. Today is most likely the best day of Greg's life, because tomorrow, next week, next month, and next year will only bring more trials and hardships.

There's no self-help book for Greg to read that will enable him or equip him to deal with all the thoughts that go through his mind each day or that will help dry the tears. He must be alone with his thoughts and process them all with his Creator. Greg's steadfast resolve to get up and keep going every day is nothing like I've ever seen in another human being. He never gives up. He keeps living life. His beloved Labradors, Nolie and Bailey, get a front-row seat to witness this resolve day in and day out.

The two of us enjoy whatever opportunities we can to hang out and do what friends do. We go out to lunch on days Greg is able, or we go for a ride in the country and stop by a cheese factory so he can load up on cheese—being a Wisconsinite, he loves cheese. Since I dislike cheese, he thinks I and all Hoosiers are weirdos. We have a few differences, but we share one very big common denominator: chronic pain, with his being the worst. In light of what he goes through every day, I'm ashamed I even mention my physical discomfort in his presence.

What Greg has shown me during the course of our friendship is, no matter how big a pity party I want to have, there are literally thousands of people who would willingly trade places with me in a second. Tens of thousands of people. So I'm challenged to look at the bigger picture of my circumstances every day. Greg's obstacles have helped me to see and to understand that I have the use of all of my body parts, and that is an enormous blessing. Sure, I have pain twenty-four hours a day, seven days a week. But I can get around and do most everything I need to do, so I have nothing to really complain about as long as I keep that in proper perspective.

Just in case you are wondering, yes, even my friend Greg realizes there are many people living in the world today who would also trade places with him in a split second. There's always someone who has suffered more or who is currently suffering more than you are, and they would love to be living your life right now.

Things could be a whole lot worse. I am blessed beyond measure.

There's not a doubt in my mind that without my twenty-seven years of chronic pain, I would not be even close to who I am today. I believe that pain is a trial, and trials test your faith. They can make you wiser, stronger, more sensitive, and a better person in the long run. Fine wine is only possible because grapes must be crushed. A fine diamond would simply be a lump of coal if not for years of pressure being applied to it. An apple tree or raspberry bush is only fruitful if dead or dying branches are pruned off. Being crushed, pressured, and pruned are all part of the process of refining our character and maturing us into fruitful human beings. Show me a productive, fruitful person in any field or discipline who has not endured trials in their life—you won't find one. Even the sycamore fig doesn't ripen into sweetness unless it is bruised.

Our human tendency is to run away from or find a quick solution to trials. That's certainly the case when physical pain is concerned. It would be abnormal to experience severe pain and never consult a physician or try to find a solution. But there comes a time when, after you've exhausted your options for a remedy or cure, you must come to terms of acceptance with it and be at peace. I don't think it's possible to truly be at peace when in pain unless you are walking alongside God. At least, that's been my experience. God has not only enabled me to be at peace but He's helped me to use it for my benefit and His glory. Max Lucado writes, "God never promises to remove us from our struggles. He does promise, however, to change the way we look at them."[7] I am convinced, absolutely convinced, I would still be a selfish, insensitive, mostly useless person had it not been for the loss of my father, the loss of my brother, and the affliction of my lower back pain happening all about the same time. It took all three blows to get the attention of the stubborn, prideful, and self-reliant man I was. I needed something bigger than anything I could fix on my own. And regardless of the number or the timing of them, trials are a part of life, so it's wise to give thought to affliction and how you will respond to it before it is thrust upon you. It's good to ponder this while sitting quietly alone in your room with only your thoughts and God, not something to run from in your busyness.

What's the lesson for me and for you? Let us be thankful in *all* circumstances and be content and at peace right where we are. Indeed, our circumstances could be worse. We can dwell on the negative and wallow in self-pity, or we can see the good and get back to living life and living it to the fullest. Often, there can be a silver lining in our trials, and at some point, we might even look back upon them as a blessing.

12

MISPLACED AFFECTIONS

In May of 2000, my older brother Gary organized a brother/ sister family reunion on a houseboat at Lake Mead near Las Vegas, Nevada. This was a different get-together for sure, as it was only my siblings who were invited for the week, not our wives or husbands or children. The purpose was to get all of us together in close quarters so we could reacquaint ourselves with one another as adults, and simply to enjoy one another's company. Three years earlier, a group of my brothers and I had gathered for a week of fishing and fellowship at Lake Buckatabon in northern Wisconsin. I think Gary found that trip to be a very enjoyable time of reconnecting, so he wanted to do it again on Lake Mead.

I was on my way, waiting to board my flight from Minneapolis to Las Vegas, when I met a fifty-eight-year-old life insurance salesman I'll call Larry, who had been divorced for nearly twenty years. He had three adult children who were all professionals, and they were each doing quite well for themselves, according to him. However, Larry came across as disappointed and angry—he lacked any sign of joy within his inner being.

On a side note, you might be wondering how in the world I learned so much personal information about Larry. It's because the encounter happened before smartphones. It was a time before everyone became so plugged into devices and stopped making eye contact; a time not all that long ago, even in this galaxy, people actually enjoyed having face-to-face conversations. Now, if a fellow passenger obviously wants to be left alone, I get it—so if you ever see me in a public place, there's no need to run and hide! But all sarcasm aside, long plane flights are ideal settings for real, meaningful conversation, and most of the time, lending an ear often invites discussion that goes far beneath the surface.

Back to Larry . . . I learned that he was not a happy camper. He had recently lost a good friend to cancer, and I could empathetically relate to his loss. He was saddened and upset about the loss of his friend, but I was shocked when he revealed what bothered him the most: his friend had purchased insurance policies from another agent, so he had missed out on all the sales commissions. Larry's words to me were, "I thought he was my friend. What kind of a friend does that to somebody, anyway? If he was a real friend, he wouldn't have cheated me out of all of those sales commissions."

Perhaps Larry was despondent over the loss of his friend and saying things he would soon regret. I hoped that was the case. Or perhaps he actually meant what he said, and he was being brutally honest with the fellow seated next to him on the flight that day. If the latter is true, then Larry certainly appears to have some priorities out of place and a misplaced love for money. I wondered what he was searching for in life that he thought would provide him happiness, meaning, and fulfillment. Was he beyond the point of pursuing greater things and simply living out the remainder of his days? I now sometimes wonder what ever became of him. Did Larry ever find joy in life?

Well, the time spent with my siblings in Nevada that week was fruitful, and I believe it achieved what we had all envisioned to one degree or another. It provided an opportunity for relationship building and for growing in grace. We lived for that week in a small living space while we physically and emotionally drew closer to one another. We shared our joys and yet only hinted at our disappointments and struggles in life. I think conversations where disappointments and struggles are revealed normally happen one-on-one, rather than in a group setting. The trip also provided me with further insight into my own heart and the heart of mankind as I reflected on my conversation with Larry.

John Newton, the author of the well-known hymn "Amazing Grace," writes, "It is proof of our depravity that good habits are much more easily lost than acquired, whereas bad habits are acquired with ease but laid aside with great difficulty."[8] This statement warrants that we pause for a moment and think deeply about this, because we know it's true within our own hearts and lives.

What about the habit of exercising regularly along with eating a healthy diet? It is certainly easier to lose this habit than it is to acquire it, don't you think? What about the bad habits of using foul language or smoking or excessive drinking or gossiping or the other things many of us wish we could discard? It isn't difficult to make those into habits, but it takes determination and work to discard them, doesn't it? We also get into the habit of looking for happiness in the wrong places or the wrong things. Our wants, desires, and goals can easily turn into misplaced affections for things that cannot profit or deliver what we had hoped.

The longer we reinforce the habit of pursuing misplaced affections the more it becomes our reality. We find ourselves searching for happiness and satisfaction in things that were never meant to provide such reward. Dr. Martyn Lloyd-Jones, who walked away from a successful medical career, declares this in one of his sermons: "God made us; we are not our own; we are his creatures and we were meant to live for his glory and his honor. Until we do, we will never know peace, we will never know happiness, we will never know joy."[9] Newton then goes on to say:

> For until we are reconciled to God, everything to which we look for satisfaction will surely disappoint us. God formed us originally for himself and has therefore given the human mind such a vastness of desire, such a thirst for happiness as he alone can answer; and therefore, until we seek our rest in him, in vain we seek it elsewhere. Neither the hurries of business or the allurements of pleasure, not the accomplishments of our wishes, can fill up the mighty void that is felt within.[10]

I believe it is in our nature to try and fill the void within us with items of our own choosing. As our fondness grows for things such as money, possessions, fame, or vocational achievement, we often select one of them to fill that hole within. But misplaced affections can never sufficiently satisfy the longing within. God formed us for Himself, and only He can fill up the hollowness within.

13

HAPPINESS VS. JOY

S ome things in life aren't rocket science. By this, I mean we would all prefer to spend time with a pleasant person rather than be in the company of a frustrated, grumpy one. None of us had to take a class or read a book to come to this conclusion—it's just common sense that it is natural to gravitate toward pleasant, fun-loving, uplifting people. I recall a line from the old movie *Harvey* starring Jimmy Stewart, "In this life you can be oh, so smart or oh, so pleasant, . . . I recommend pleasant."

We'd all recommend pleasant, right? There's a difference between genuinely pleasant people and folks who fake it—you cannot fake pleasant! Our true makeup will always come to the surface at some point. Don't get me wrong, we all have bad moments and bad days—real life isn't all lollipops and birthday balloons. But we can tell when a friend, coworker, or family member is feeling defeated by the trials of life, which affects how pleasant or unpleasant they are when we're around them.

When I visited with Larry that day on the flight to Las Vegas, it was obvious he was carrying a lot of frustration and disappointment within him. He was not a pleasant person. I'm not sure how he came to that point in life, but I'm certain he wasn't riding his bike one day at the age of ten and thought to himself, *Hmmm, I want to be a frustrated, grumpy person when I grow up.* No, I'm certain that wasn't the case. It wasn't his childhood dream to turn out like that—it just happened little by little by little. That's the way it usually happens.

Being pleasant or unpleasant leads me to the two states of mind we all face: happiness and joy—and there is a difference between the two. I believe *happiness* is a temporary state of mind that's conditioned on the right circumstances, whereas *joy* is something more long-term and sustaining no matter your circumstances. *Joy* is a feeling of great pleasure, delight, jubilation, gladness, exhilaration, and elation, whereas *happiness* is contentment, pleasure, satisfaction, or cheerfulness. On the surface, both joy and happiness seem to be very similar, but there is a significant difference between the two: joy is sustaining, whereas happiness is fleeting or short-lived.

Happiness is triggered by external stimuli based on an event, a thought, a person . . . a grape Nehi soda pop, or a favorite candy bar. Happiness is not sustainable, whereas joy certainly is. The Green Bay Packers winning a football game on Sunday makes me extremely happy and a delightful person to be around, but the happiness quickly dissipates when they lose to the Minnesota Vikings at Lambeau Field the following Sunday. Happiness is fleeting, so while pursuing and experiencing it is good, it cannot be our end-all purpose in life. If it is, then we'll experience disappointment after disappointment. We'll end up living a life without sustaining joy.

Joy comes from a place within where there is peace that

surpasses all understanding. That means you can have joy no matter what you are facing. Joy is with you when you get out of bed in the morning, even though your body aches and says it doesn't want to. Joy sustains you when your spouse appears to pay more attention to other things or people than he or she does to you. Joy can still be there when you take your sick child to the doctor and still there is no answer or medication for the ongoing pain in his or her abdomen. I agree with Jimmy Stewart's character: I too would prefer to be oh, so pleasant, rather than oh, so smart. So how and where do we find true joy?

C. S. Lewis authored a book with a great title, *Surprised by Joy*. He wrote this book to describe a time in his life when he transitioned from atheism to Christianity and thus found a sustaining, supernatural joy in his life. Lewis is mostly known for his other books, such as *The Chronicles of Narnia*, *The Screwtape Letters*, or *Mere Christianity*, but I am particularly fond of *Surprised by Joy*, if not solely for the title. Many years after authoring this book, Lewis was married late in life to Joy Gresham. I think it's coincidental and quite ironic that one man had two remarkable life-changing encounters with joy and Joy.

In his book *Don't Waste Your Life*, John Piper expounds upon his discovery that "God being glorified, and God being enjoyed are not separate categories. God's aim in history was to fully display his glory and God's aim was that his people delight in him with all of their heart." Piper goes on to say,

This was the great coming together for me, the breakthrough. What was life about? What was it for? Why do I exist? Why am I here? Am I here to be happy or to glorify God? Unspoken for years, there was in me the feeling that these two were at odds. Either you glorify God or pursue happiness. One seemed absolutely right; the other seemed absolutely inevitable. And that was why I was confused and frustrated for so long.

Compounding the problem was that many who seemed to emphasize the glory of God in their thinking did not seem to enjoy him very much. And many who seemed to enjoy God most were defective in their thinking about his glory. But now here was the greatest mind in early America, Jonathan Edwards, saying that God's purpose for my life was that I have a passion for God's glory and that I have a passion for my joy in that glory, and that these two are one passion. When I saw this, I knew at last what a wasted life would be and how to avoid it. God created me and you to live with a single, all-embracing, all-transforming passion, namely a passion to glorify God by enjoying and display-ing his supreme excellence in all the spheres of life.[11]

As a result of this revelation and the bringing-together of joy and glorifying God, Piper coined a signature motto to live by: "God is most glorified in us when we are most satisfied in Him."[12] I think this line is worth repeating. "God is most glorified in us when we are most satisfied in Him." I find that one of the key words here is *satisfied*. Satisfaction isn't fleeting. The word evokes contentment; a state of being pleased or fulfilled. It appears that satisfaction and joy are closely knit together, doesn't it? While happiness comes and goes, joy and satisfaction are sustainable. According to Piper, being satisfied in God and possessing peace, contentment, and joy is a function of living for the glory of God. We must cling to this source of joy with all of our heart, soul, mind and strength.

Happiness can be replaced with a state of sadness, discouragement, or despondency in an instant. However, joy is constant and never disappoints. Not unlike Lewis and Piper, I too was perhaps searching for happiness, but instead was surprised to discover joy. Joy, unspeakable joy, is to be sought after and cherished once found. Larry, the disappointed and frustrated insurance agent, did not exhibit this unspeakable joy. My hope is that he made a turnaround somewhere along his way and pursued the Author of such joy.

To know and possess joy unspeakable is a gift available to everyone who seeks it. Peace, joy, and contentment are all elements of a fulfilled life. In his book *Jesus Among Other Gods*, Ravi Zacharias writes, "If I am to be fulfilled, I must pursue a will that is greater than mine. A fulfilled life is one that has the will of God as its focus, not the appetite of the flesh."[13]

In other words, a life lived where I am the center of attention is contrary to what Zacharias is describing. Perhaps a fulfilled life looks much different than a typical life. Perhaps this is where Larry and I both erred for a good portion of our lives. The good news is, once we come to this realization, we can get a fresh start. Author Max Lucado writes, "We pray for a hand that will enter the dark caverns of our world and do for us the one thing we can't do for ourselves . . . make us right again."[14]

I believe we all long to hear that voice inside—that voice that awakens us to the purpose for which we were given life in the first place. Deep down within our being, we all want life to have greater meaning and significance; we want to live a life that matters. We want our lives to matter and to have purpose. We want to do something significant and live with forward focus rather than settle and react to whatever life throws our way. We want to leave a legacy. We want to do something or be someone who made a real difference and contribution in life.

I had the opportunity to visit Nairobi, Kenya in 2010. While there, I joined Bishop Moses and his family to do life together in a place far different from the comforts of the world I was accustomed to. Even though I was there for less than two weeks, I was able to get to know and enjoy several beautiful, spirited Kenyans who were simply marvelous people. We shared so very much in common, even though we lived on opposite sides of the globe. I also discovered that they longed for the same things Americans long for: happiness, joy, purpose, meaning, and fulfillment. But first and foremost, they longed for the necessities of life that I and many of us take for granted: food, clean water, and shelter.

Many of the Africans I met lived in the slums of Kibera. There are no living conditions in the United States that compare. One very hot day, Bishop Moses escorted me and my American friend Josh through the streets of a Nairobi slum, and I observed people who had a zeal for life. I saw people caring for their loved ones as best they could. They were an industrious people; many had street stands selling anything and everything imaginable, from goat's milk and eggs to shoes. I also witnessed living conditions I had only seen in television documentaries. These people were no longer just a passing moment on the TV screen or in a magazine photo—they were real, live, breathing people. The stench in the air from rotting food, human waste, and garbage was an odor that penetrated my senses to a point I will never, ever forget. It reminded me of an open garbage dump where we took our trash when I was a child, yet people were living in this one. I witnessed this again on a subsequent trip to Guatemala, where people not only went to the dump to scavenge and seek food or anything else of value, but they actually set up shelters and lived at the dump site.

Several of the folks who lived in the Nairobi slum attended the same church that I attended earlier in the week. Bernard was one of the pastors there, and he also lived in the slum. But when I saw him that Sunday morning, he wore his Sunday-best clothes and his shoes were shiny. I never would have guessed that he and his family lived in such deplorable conditions. I recall visiting with Bernard following the Sunday service and he was, of course, asking me many questions about life in my country. He had also shared that he was a machinist in a nearby manufacturing facility. That sounded like a pretty good job to me and, since it was a skilled position, should pay fairly well. Upon my inquiry, Bernard explained that, "Yes, it is a good job, but employers here are not trustworthy." He went on to say that once you leave a position at one factory to take a better paying position somewhere else, the new employer will only pay you the new, higher wage for the first month or so. As soon as enough time passed for your former employer to fill your old position, the new employer would reduce your pay to only what it took to keep you around. And they don't pay you weekly, but only when they think you are ready to leave and go elsewhere. Bernard said this is very common since there are few to no employment laws.

Bernard could see that I was dumbfounded at such poor treatment of the workers. He assumed that was the case everywhere in the world, but I assured him that in America, we have laws and agencies that enforce those laws on behalf of mistreated employees. His eyes opened wide with such awe and wonder, and then he exclaimed, "I must come to your country, Brother Greg, I must come to your country!" I quickly explained to him that it wasn't a good time for manufacturing in our country, as we were going through a rough economic recession and that many workers had been laid off from their jobs and were living only on a government-provided unemployment check. He looked up at me curiously and asked, "What is an unemployment check?" I went on to explain that each employer pays an unemployment tax to the government, and if or when employees are laid off work, the money is available to provide for employees when they are out of work. He looked at me in utter amazement and asked, "Are you saying that your government pays people when they do not work?" I said, "No, no it's not like that, it's . . ." And that's when I realized and said, "Yes, I guess that's what we do in our country, but it's only for a specific number of weeks."

Bernard again looked up at me with a big, bright smile on his face and said, "Brother Greg, I must come to your country!" That's when I really had my Dorothy from *The Wizard of Oz* moment. No, I wasn't in Kansas anymore. No, this wasn't make-believe; it was very real.

Bernard is no different than you or me. We're all searching for something better in life, whether it is better living conditions, greater or more secure income, or other earthly things. Regardless of what side of the world we live on, the human condition is the same. Once our basic needs are met, we all long to live a life that matters; a life with purpose that is fulfilled and sustained with joy. We see this played out before us time and time again, don't we? We see this search for significance, or even hear it played out through the song lyrics of contemporary performing artists like Ricky Skaggs in the song "Mosaic," as he sings of wanting desperately to leave his mark in this world and really matter to someone—to be remembered for something worthwhile.

We see this search on a simple scale, as in a song like "Mosaic" and we see it played out on a grand scale in great people like William Wilberforce and Abraham Lincoln. There is a desire seeded deeply within most of us to do something that matters in the bigger scheme of life and to be remembered for it. While we may never be a Wilberforce or a Lincoln, or even a performer like Ricky Skaggs, I believe we all long to be remembered for something of significance.

I think that's why I like to take the time to read the many roadside markers across our country. They relay a subtle message to the rest of us normal folks that, in this spot, another normal, everyday person just like you and me did something that was worthy to be remembered. Did you know that Nickolaus Gerber (1836–1903) learned cheese making as he grew up in Switzerland, then later immigrated to New York and founded that state's first Limburger cheese factory? After hearing reports of successful dairy cow farms in Green County, Wisconsin (near my home), Gerber moved here and, in 1868, established Wisconsin's very first Limburger cheese factory. After 130 years, it remains the last operating Limburger cheese factory in the United States.

Wisconsin also has a roadside marker titled Wisconsin's First Aviator. The nation's first commercially built aeroplane was assembled and flown in Rock County, Wisconsin on November 4, 1909 by Arthur P. Warner. Warner was Wisconsin's first pilot, and self-taught at that. He was the eleventh American to pilot a powered aircraft and the first in the US to buy an aircraft for business use.

And way back in 1835, Father Samuel Mazzuchelli, a Dominican missionary, came to the lead-mining region of southwest Wisconsin and established schools and began preparing teachers for the children of the settlers. In 1847, he formed Wisconsin's first teaching sisterhood, the Sinsinawa Dominican Sisters. At Benton, Wisconsin he founded St. Clara Female Academy and taught science with the earliest laboratory instruments. He went on to design and build twenty churches in the upper Mississippi Valley.[15] Gerber, Warner, and Father Mazzuchelli were normal people just like you and me who are remembered for living fruitful and productive lives.

Whether it be carving our name into a tree, having our name and story inscribed upon a roadside marker, penning a love letter to your spouse, child or grandchild, or whatever worthy accomplishment that could be listed—all are just by-products of a life lived with purpose. My sister-in-law recently asked me, "Do you have hobbies to keep you occupied once you retire?" I certainly understood why she asked the question, since most retired Americans fill their time with hobbies and such. Hobbies are great, entertainment is great, vacations are great, watching your favorite television show or going out to a movie, play or concert can all be very worthwhile ventures, but a life filled with diversions such as these is seldom a purpose-driven or fulfilled life. We want our lives to matter, not just be occupied while time passes by. Life is a gift, and it's important not to squander it.

Over the years, I have sadly witnessed many reasonably healthy adults spend hour after hour staring at a television screen, wasting away yet another day. In Dr. John Dunlop's book *Finishing Well to the Glory of God*, he states, "When we pursue pleasures in lesser things, we forfeit the opportunity to find our greatest fulfillment in the greatness of God, and we will never ultimately be satisfied."[16] It has been my experience and is my belief that joy is at the heart of living a fruitful life. We can make all the New Year's resolutions, read all the trending books, or try every Ten-Ways-to-a-Better-Life program available, yet we will still fall short of living a truly fulfilled life unless life-changing, sustaining joy is at the core of it. Let us not fall short by pursuing pleasures in lesser things and missing the greatness of God.

14

SPIRITUAL REWARDS IN NATURE

There are two spiritual dangers in not owning a farm. One is the danger of supposing that breakfast comes from the grocery, and the other that heat comes from the furnace. To avoid the first danger, one should plant a garden, preferably where there is no grocer to confuse the issue. To avoid the second, one should lay a good split of oak on the andirons, preferably where there is no furnace, and let it warm his shins while a February blizzard tosses the trees outside.[17]

The renowned conservationist Aldo Leopold wrote these words in 1949, a period that is a bit different from the times in which we live today. Few, if any, actually have a vegetable garden, a wood stove, or a fireplace in our home that functions as a source of heat. Those current realities aside, I still find it quite beneficial and therapeutic to reflect on the "two spiritual dangers" that Leopold has brought to light for us.

There's a part of me that wants to grow what I eat. There's also a part of me that wants to cut and split my own firewood so

I can have a roaring fire in the fireplace if I want. Heaven forbid, if Vicky and I lost our electric power during the winter, I could at least make certain we would stay warm and cozy, despite the fact we wouldn't be able to recharge our smartphones. I think a lot of men share the same primal desire deep within them to provide for the basic and essential needs of their family. That's why I believe that Leopold is on to something when he states, "There are two spiritual dangers in not owning a farm." Without ever being able to experience the struggles and the rewards associated with growing our own food, I do believe we might be missing out on one of life's essential elements.

Our culture has changed greatly since Leopold penned these words. Most of us no longer live in rural settings where we have enough land to plant a large garden, nor do we have the necessary space for farm animals. Vicky and I have been blessed, however, because we do have enough land to do exactly that. Soon after purchasing our forty acres, we began planting apple trees in the vicinity just north of the spot where we would eventually build our new home. Between the orchard and the building site, we also planted several rows of red and black raspberry plants. We decided not to plant a vegetable garden until after we actually built our house on the property a few years later. Having grown up on a farm, I knew very well that growing Christmas trees, apple trees, and raspberries was not all cupcakes and birthday balloons, but the past twenty-five years of living away from the farm sure had dampened my sense of reality.

We initially planted seventeen apple trees in our orchard. After a few years of caring for the trees, picking apples, cleaning apples, bagging apples, raking up rotten apples, and giving away apples to food pantries and every person or family that we knew under the sun, I finally came to the conclusion that we simply had too many apple trees. Having them seemed as if it should be a Hallmark-movie moment, where the apples turn ripe at just the perfect time, they never pile up underneath the trees and attract thousands of yellow jackets, and all of your neighbors are happy to receive your bounty, but it wasn't. Heck, our neighbors run inside when they see us coming over with yet another bushel or bag of apples! We cannot give them away fast enough.

Since this realization, I began to cut down and remove one apple tree each year. That has been my pattern for about the past ten years now. Currently we have three full-size, two semi-dwarf, and two dwarf apple trees. I think that still might be too many, but only time will tell. My wife just shakes her head every time I cut down and haul away another tree, but then again, she really likes Hallmark movies. I've found that real life isn't like a Hallmark movie, however, and a man has to do what a man has to do. Thank you for bearing with me as I share my apple tree reality show with you.

All joking aside, owning a small farm and growing things is a blessing indeed. Aldo Leopold is right: we miss out on something very important for our inner being the further we get away from the basic, simple things in life. It's very rewarding, healthy, and good to grow your own food, but it's also important to understand that food just doesn't pop into being without someone somewhere sacrificing a lot of effort and energy to make it happen. Heating your home with firewood is a whole lot of work, but cutting trees and splitting, gathering, and stacking firewood are all worth-while and therapeutic activities. By the way, Hallmark movies also make handling firewood look romantic—the flames you see in fireplace scenes are something like I've never seen or experienced in real life.

Another way to put food in the freezer and then on the table is deer hunting. It's an outdoor activity that not only helps me connect with nature but also affords my mind the opportunity to think endlessly about important things that matter to me. I actually enjoy other types of hunting more, but white-tailed deer hunting in the upper Midwest is primarily a sit-still-and-wait form of therapy. Oh, you can stroll leisurely and as quietly as possible through the woods or marsh, but your chances of actually seeing and harvesting an animal are much greater if you position your tree stand in a tree with a wide view, then sit or stand there quietly. Once a deer walks by, you have a choice to make: do I harvest this deer, or do I let it walk by and wait for another, larger one? It sounds simple, but there's a lot more to it than what I've described. There's much more to hunting than simply killing a deer, and I love the whole process.

For me and most other hunters I know, simply being outside in our natural environment to observe nature in action and to be alone with nothing but your thoughts and whatever God might whisper to you is a satisfaction like no other. It's not uncommon to sit up in a tree for hours on end and never even see a deer, but you don't mind because you're just glad to have been outside in such peaceful surroundings. It's time and space that allows you to escape the hustle and bustle of life. There are no distractions, no nagging bosses. Instead, you can watch grey squirrels do their treetop acrobatics and play with one another for hours. Or you might end up watching a busy chipmunk gathering food or get an up-close view of a nuthatch hopping down the tree trunk just a few inches from your eyes. A wild turkey leaving the roost at daybreak or a raccoon wobbling along the ground beneath you are also sights that will put a smile on your face. There are so many sights and sounds to enjoy, whether you ever see a deer or not. But mainly, there's time to be alone with your thoughts and with the God who created you. It's what makes you want to keep coming back, whether for another long day or even for only a few hours. The experience calls you back time and again.

While Vicky isn't as obsessed with the outdoors as I am, she also shares a fondness for God's creation and is more than willing to go with me for a stroll in our woodlot or through our field of Christmas trees. Sometimes we'll visit a nearby state park for some hiking and sightseeing. God created much for us to enjoy, and we never tire of experiencing all that has been laid before us. Thinking on it, I would add to Leopold's axiom of spiritual dangers by also incorporating, "There are spiritual dangers in not visiting the American West as often as you are physically and financially able."

You are already aware of my affinity for the American West, as that is where I spent a month during my search for direction for the second half of my life. It is also a place I had visited three times prior to that occasion and a place where Vicky and I have vacationed on three occasions since. I'm almost certain this year has a hiking trip planned to the badlands of North Dakota and Theodore Roosevelt National Park.

I truly believe that anyone wired to enjoy the outdoors and feel a spiritual connection to the wonder of nature actually robs themselves of a blessing when they fall victim to busyness and don't set aside time to simply go outdoors. Whether camping and hiking in Glacier National Park, sightseeing in Yellowstone, or exploring the wonders of Arizona and New Mexico, there is a great balm for your inner being that awaits you. I encourage you to escape to such places as often as you are able to be alone with your thoughts and your Creator. I believe there is a spiritual danger in not doing so.

15

THE FOUNTAIN OF LIFE

Upon ending, I want to ponder the subtitle of this book: *An Ordinary Man's Search for Meaning.* There's certainly a lot of supporting evidence that I am exactly that—an ordinary, average, run-of-the-mill man. So aside from all the musings about seeing the grandeur of the American West, having too many apple trees, making a drastic, mid-life career change, along with my endless affection for candy bars, what's the point of it all? *So what if I can now afford to buy any candy bar?* Most everyone reading this book can afford one too. You also might be thinking, *So what if Greg believes in a God-centered worldview? Simply believing that God exists doesn't make everything perfect. What does this mean for me?* Let me try to bring it all together the very best I can.

Yes, I am just an ordinary man, but I have lived an examined life. I am a thinking man, and I naturally question everything. I'm not an academic scholar or a peer-reviewed, published author, but I have an above-average understanding of the major religions, along with their associated worldviews. I also have academic and vocational training in the life sciences, plus a thirst for knowledge of the natural order of things. And to top it off, I have lived sixty-four years with my eyes, ears, and mind wide open every step of the way. I have read and studied the works of many well-known scholars who have "PhD" printed after their names who have come to the same conclusion I have: an accurate worldview must have coherence.

Our origin, meaning, morality, destiny—they all must fit together and correspond to reality and be without contradictions. I must have reasonable and noncontradictory answers to the four most critical questions: what is the origin of life; what gives meaning in life; who defines morality in life; what is the final destiny in life? In my opinion, Christianity is the only religious system and worldview that adequately addresses those questions. Ravi Zacharias helped me come to this conclusion many years ago during my search. Other religious systems or worldviews may reasonably address one or two, but Christianity is the only faith that adequately addresses and provides coherence to all four of them.

I have concluded that a life lived without God at the center is a wasted, unfruitful, and unfulfilled life. Conversely, a life lived where God has His proper place—above all else—is a fruitful life, a purpose-driven life, a fulfilled life, and a joyful life. It is vitally important to me that you fully understand that your life matters—and *you matter to God.* Without this understanding, life is truly meaningless. Max Lucado writes:

Shouldn't we face the truth? If we do not acknowledge God, we are flotsam in the universe. At best we are developed animals. At worst we are rearranged space dust. In the final analysis, secularists have only one answer to the question, "What is the meaning of Life?" Their answer is,

"We don't know." With God in your world, you are no accident or incident; you are a gift to the world, a divine work of art, signed by God.[18]

In conclusion, I reiterate the title of this book: *I Can Buy Any Candy Bar*. Wow! Let me pinch myself and say that again out loud: "Now, I can buy any candy bar!" When I was a youngster of modest means, I wasn't sure if this day would ever come. I can afford to buy any candy bar at any time of the day that I choose. In fact, I can afford to buy anything that I want. I can buy any toy I want, like an ATV, a motorcycle, or an RV. I can buy any car I want, or any vacation, or even whatever house I want. Yes, I have been blessed beyond measure, more than I could have ever possibly hoped for or imagined. Yes, I have the means to purchase absolutely anything that I want.

You might be thinking to yourself, *Hey, wait just a minute. I thought this guy said he was an ordinary man of average means. Doesn't he just have a part-time consulting business and a small Christmas tree farm that provides only part-time income? How can he afford to buy any house or absolutely anything else he wants?* Those are excellent questions, and this is my answer: I can now buy any candy bar, at any time, along with anything else I *want*. You see, the *want* has changed dramatically! I've reached a point in life where my wants aren't what they used to be, nor are they typical of a successful man living in America. I can afford to buy anything I want, but the catch is, I don't want an extravagant home or a luxury car or an over-the-top boat. The want has changed. Yes, the want has changed and only God can author such dramatic change. I started out in life looking for a candy bar anytime I wanted; I instead discovered God, who satisfies all of my appetites and more than adequately provides for all of my needs and desires.

Finding God and following Him doesn't mean a life free of difficulties, trials, or pain. But experiencing God in a personal relationship changes the way you look at and experience trials in life. And you might ask, "Does God find me, or do I search for God?" I believe the best, most concise explanation of seeking God was written by John Stott:

"In the beginning God." These are the first four words of the Bible and they supply the key which opens our understanding of the Bible as a whole. They tell us the religion of the Bible is a religion of the initiative of God. . . . Before man existed, God acted. Before man stirs himself to seek God, God has sought man. In the Bible we do not see man groping after God; we see God reaching after man. . . . The Bible reveals a God, who, long before it even occurs to man to turn to Him, while man is still shrouded in darkness and sunk in sin, takes the initiative, rises from His Throne, lays aside His glory and stoops to seek until He finds him. . . . The sovereign, anticipating activity of God is seen in many ways. . . . . God has taken the initiative in creation, He has taken initiative in revelation and He has taken initiative in salvation. . . . These statements of God's initiative in three different spheres form a summary of the religion in the

Bible. . . . If God has spoken, He has the greatest word to the world in Jesus Christ. If God has acted, His noblest act is the redemption of the world through Jesus Christ. God has both spoken and acted in Jesus Christ. . . . This is the gospel or good news. . . . The record and the interpretation of the divine words and deeds are found in the Bible. And there they will remain unless we play our part. What God has said and done belongs to history, but it must pass from history and into our present experience. It must come out of the Bible and into our lives. . . . We must seek. God has sought us. God is still seeking us. We must seek God. "Seek and you will find" (Matthew 7:7). If we do not seek, we shall never find. . . . God is not an ogre, playing hide-and-seek with us in the trackless jungle of the heart and mind, but He requires us to seek Him. He desires to be found. We must seek diligently. We must overcome our natural sloth and apply ourselves earnestly to the task.[19]

God is the source of all contentment, love, joy, peace, patience, kindness, goodness, faithfulness, gentleness, and self-control. When we choose to live life apart from Him, we miss out on the many blessings that He has intended for us. Not only do we miss out on the blessings, but we end up living a life that is missing an elevated sense of purpose and fruitfulness. Essentially, we are settling for less—far less than what we were created for. We were created to glorify God and to enjoy Him forever. This is impossible until we meet with Him and have a life-changing encounter and personal relationship with the living God.

Vicky and I arrived at the infant stage of this discovery and acted upon it back in 1994 when we purchased our land and started a Christmas tree farm. The main reason we started Winterberry Christmas Trees was to do our part to introduce the visitors who came to our farm to the person of Jesus Christ. Most often, people come for the experience of cutting a real tree with their family or friends. Many folks don't know that Christ is at the center of the Christmas season, and if they do, they've lost sight of it because the celebration has been so materialized and filled with busyness.

Vicky and I take pleasure in honoring God as we share Him with all who visit and work with us. It is a high priority that each of our helpers be joyful in their speech and actions while keeping Christ at the forefront of why we celebrate Christmas. "Merry Christmas!" is proclaimed over and over as we serve our guests. We celebrate Christmas because Jesus—the Lamb of God—was born to us here on earth. Without His birth, there would be no Christmas to celebrate. The gift of Jesus Christ is God's greatest gift in the history of the world. Because He lives, we may live also.

I have fallen for God hook, line, and sinker, and I cannot imagine living life without Him at the center of everything I do. I've learned that life lived alongside the God who created me for a divine purpose is a living romance with the Author of Life. Yes, you read that correctly. A guy actually used the word *romance* to describe something that matters more than anything. We're all enticed by romance, whether we choose to acknowledge it or not. And a living, breathing, real-life romance with God Himself is the ultimate romance. That's why I continue to want to live yet another day despite the many physical ailments that plague my body. I am certain that John Newton, who also suffered great physical discomfort late in life, shared my reasoning when he penned these words in a letter to a dear friend: "I trust the chief reason why I should wish my life to be prolonged is that I may employ more of my breath in His Praise."[20]

God is to be sought after, my dear friends, God is to be sought after. And once you do and have met Him, He is to be glorified through a lifestyle of worship. He is a never-ending fountain—the Fountain of Life that satisfies more than all the pleasures on earth combined. Yes, this Fountain is even more satisfying to me now than my favorite candy bar was to me as a child. Once we drink of the living water from this Fountain, we are never thirsty again. I share the same affection for the Fountain of Life as does the unknown author of this short prayer.

> And let me not lay my pipe
> too short of the Fountain,
> never touching the Eternal Spring,
> never drawing down water from above.[21]

The author of this prayer testifies to the greatness and the importance of having the Fountain as the central pivot-point in his life. Oh, if he were to "lay his pipe too short of the Fountain," what despair there would be. How tragic it would be for him never to drink from the Eternal Spring, never to be nourished, never to be refreshed and never to be sustained by Living Water from above. He is praying that God would not allow him to make such a blunder and miss out on the main thing.

Make certain that your home is near the Fountain. See to it that you work close to the Fountain. Take vacations alongside the Fountain. Play near the Fountain. Search for it, find it, and never lose sight of it once you discover it. Put down your roots and lay your pipe close to the Fountain. If you don't, you will have squandered a divine opportunity; you will have missed out on the gift of living a joyful, fulfilling life. You will have lived apart from the Eternal Spring, the Fountain of Life.

God asks us to abide in Him and do life with Him in our thoughts and our actions. When we do, He promises to nourish and refresh us continually. He encourages us to be yoked with Him and to learn from Him. He promises, "Whoever abides in me and I in him, he it is that bears much fruit, for apart from me you can do nothing" (John 15:5). Let us not miss out on such a wonderful promise. God is the perfect Promise Keeper, and He who promises is faithful. He will surely do it!

Yes, there is more to life than your favorite candy bar.

EPILOGUE

I have read many times that journaling is a great and worthwhile discipline, but I seldom do. Why? If I'm totally honest, there are simply other things I'd rather be doing. And if I were a faithful journal keeper, I could simply supply a list of activities of what God has done through me since I began to do life alongside of Him. But since I'm not, I'll go by memory.

The purpose of this is to simply provide you with a *glimpse* of what God is capable of doing—the changes He can make in you—once you put Him on the throne of your life. This is not to boast of anything I have accomplished on my own, but to boast of what Christ has done in me. Someone else's list will look totally different from mine, and that's the way it should be. This is not all-encompassing, nor is it intended to be. The purpose here is to give you an idea of how I availed myself to be used by God more often and more fully since leaving my corporate job. If I had not made that life change, this list would look very different. My life has been and is still very full, but not with the typical busyness so many people find themselves in. I count the time invested here as significant—eternally significant from His point of view. I am humbled and blessed because of it.

- Set apart a meaningful amount of time each day to actively grow in grace and knowledge of God. Daily Bible reading, along with devotional reading, meditation, and prayer.
- Go before the throne of God in prayer to intercede for friends, coworkers, loved ones, and new acquaintances.
- Have one-on-one meetings and counseling sessions with friends and new acquaintances to lend an ear and be an encouragement.
- Arrange for small group meetings in our home to teach, to encourage, and to learn from one another.
- Participate in ongoing mentoring relationships.
- Transport folks to scheduled, or sometimes unscheduled, doctor appointments, surgeries, dialysis, etc.
- Make in-home visits with folks on the fringe of society and with shut-ins to practice the ministry of presence.
- Visit seniors in nursing homes and assisted living facilities to read with them, sit with them, pray with them, or just be present with them.
- Gift money to folks in need.
- Deliver Meals-on-Wheels to seniors and shut-ins.
- Pay for and make home repairs for folks in need, e.g. new roof, water heater, or furnace.
- Install storm windows, wash windows, clean house, mow lawns, rake leaves, trim trees and shrubs, clean gutters, and shovel snow for widows and senior citizens.
- Help senior citizens move out of their home and into an apartment, assisted living facility, or nursing home.
- Care for elderly person suffering with dementia, but who has no children or immediate family.

- Pay for a non-family member's college education.
- Serve as Missions & Outreach leader through our local church.
- Donate used vehicles from our small business to families in need.
- Provide fresh garden and orchard produce to the local food pantry and to folks in need.
- Prepare and serve a home-cooked meal once a month at our local food and clothes pantry.
- Donate proceeds from the preparation and sale of raspberry jam at our Christmas tree shop to a global disaster relief agency.
- Provide financial support to missionaries in foreign lands.
- Deliver fresh Christmas wreaths to low-income residents and senior citizens.
- Pay overdue utility bills and purchase a cell phone plan for folks in need.
- Purchase new furniture or bedding for folks in need.
- Pay for car repairs for folks in need.
- Watch children while Mom or Dad go for a job interview or take care of other critical needs.
- Since I spent a good deal of time traveling and staying in motels, I'd leave a handwritten note of encouragement each morning for the housekeeper, along with a monetary gift to bless them.
- Provide financial assistance for two children living in Bart-waba, Kenya.
- While dining out, pay for lunch or dinner for large families or senior citizens.

- Pay for groceries for the person in front of me in the checkout line, especially if I notice they are buying only essential items.
- Purchase a grocery gift card and provide it anonymously to a family in need.
- Transport a person to the dentist and pay for essential dental work.
- Take in a homeless person to live in our home while they sober up or until they chose to live back on the street.

Oh, what a glorious day it will be to stand before God on that great day and hear the words, "Well done good and faithful servant. You have been faithful over a little; I will set you over much. Enter into the joy of your master" (Matthew 25:23).

May God do great things in you and through you. Dream big!

NOTES

1. Ravi Zacharias, *Can Man Live Without God* (Dallas, TX: Word Publishing, 1994), 113.
2. Blaise Pascal, *The Wager and Other Selections from the Pensées* (Washington, DC: The Trinity Forum Reading, 1995), 23 (136).
3. Pascal, 19 (68 and 326).
4. Pascal, 29 (160).
5. Peter Kreeft, *Christianity for Modern Pagans* (San Francisco: Ignatius Press, 1993), quoted in Blaise Pascal, *The Wager and Other Selections from the Pensées* (Washington, DC: The Trinity Forum Reading, 1995), 29.
6. John W. Gardner, *Self-Renewal* (New York: W. W. Norton & Company, Ltd., 1995), 97.
7. Max Lucado, *Just Like Jesus: Learning to Have a Heart Like His* (Nashville, TN: Thomas Nelson, 2008), https://www.goodreads.com/author/quotes/2737.Max_Lucado?page=6.
8. Josiah Bull, *Letters of John Newton with Biographical Sketches and Notes* (Carlisle, PA: The Banner of Truth Trust, 2007), 164, 136.

9. "Jesus Christ and Him Crucified," hsinchureformed.org, http://www.hsinchureformed.org/Data/Articles/A4.pdf.

10. Josiah Bull, *Letters of John Newton with Biographical Sketches and Notes* (Carlisle, PA: The Banner of Truth Trust, 2007), 201–202.

11. John Piper, *Don't Waste Your Life* (Wheaton, IL: Crossway, 2009), 28, 31.

12. "God Is Most Glorified in Us When We Are Most Satisfied in Him," Desiring God Ministries, updated October 13, 2012, https://www.desiringgod.org/messages/god-is-most-glorified-in-us-when-we-are-most-satisfied-in-him.

13. Ravi Zacharias, *Jesus Among Other Gods* (Nashville, TN: Word Publishing, 2000), 85.

14. Max Lucado, *The Applause of Heaven* (Nashville, TN: W Publishing Group, 1999), 97.

15. Wisconsin Historical Society, last modified August 17, 2020, https://www.wisconsinhistory.org/Records/Article/CS3210.

16. John Dunlop, MD, *Finishing Well to the Glory of God* (Wheaton, IL: Crossway, 2011), 65.

17. Aldo Leopold, *A Sand County Almanac* (New York: Oxford University Press, 1968), 6.

18. Max Lucado, *In the Grip of Grace* (Nashville, TN: Word Publishing, 1996), 30.

19. John R. W. Stott, *Basic Christianity* (Downers Grove, IL: InterVarsity Press, 1971), 11–16.

20. Josiah Bull, *Letters of John Newton with Biographical Sketches and Notes* (Carlisle, PA: The Banner of Truth Trust, 2007), 136.

21. Arthur Bennett, *The Valley of Vision* (Carlisle, PA: The Banner of Truth Trust, 2013), 123.